THE
RICH
AND
THE
POOR

A Study of the Economics of Rising Expectations

THE
RICH
AND
THE
POOR

by Robert Theobald

Clarkson N. Potter, Inc./Publisher

NEW YORK

Library of Congress Card Catalog Number: 60-11494

DESIGNED BY HARVEY SATENSTEIN

MANUFACTURED IN THE UNITED STATES OF AMERICA BY

BOOK CRAFTSMEN ASSOCIATES, INC., NEW YORK

First Edition

Contents

To

IRENE

A Preface

Primarily for Social Scientists

THIS PREFACE, UNLIKE the rest of the book, is addressed primarily to social scientists—particularly economists—and not to the general reader. It should not be necessary to express a hope that the social scientist will not restrict his reading to these pages and that the non-specialist will be stimulated, after reading the whole book, to return here for a brief outline of the basic assumptions underlying the argument. I cannot and indeed would not want to claim that the rest is bedtime reading; however, it is my belief that the argument should be understandable by everybody even if they have no training in the social sciences. Because my purpose is to produce a panoramic picture of a vast subject, readers who are expert in any of the fields treated will feel that more space should have been given to their specialty. However, the result of such lengthening would have been to make the book unsuitable for its purpose.

My argument could not have been based on the neoclassical economic framework, for it is generally agreed that this does not reflect present world conditions, and that its static assumptions are inappropriate when worldwide economic growth is taking place. The theory lives on, however, despite continuous challenges, and it has demonstrated its continuing vitality by absorbing Keynesian theory to form what is often called a Keynesian-neoclassical-synthesis. The whole argument of this book challenges its validity, showing that policies based on its assumptions will often aggravate rather than cure present problems.

The validity—and indeed the very possibility of a satisfactory economic synthesis based on present assumptions would be challenged by many of the best economic analysts. Nevertheless its existence is formally claimed in the economic text most widely used in America. "Repeatedly throughout I have set forth what I call a 'grand neoclassical synthesis,' This is a synthesis of the valid core of modern income determination with the classical economic principles. Its basic tenet is this: Solving the vital problems of monetary and fiscal policy by the tools of income analysis will *validate* and bring back into relevance the classical verities."*

The basic theoretical departure in this work is the recognition of a fundamental contradiction in neoclassical economics, which contains *two different* theories about the effect of an increase in the quantity of income received on the amount of work carried out. One assumption (profit maximization) is based on a belief that an increase in income will not alter the amount of work done; the other (the backward-sloping supply curve of labor) suggests that an increase in income *will* lead to a change in the number of hours worked. These two assumptions correspond to two totally different sets of social attitudes—in one, work is considered vitally

---

Economics, 4th Ed. Paul A. Samuelson. McGraw-Hill, New York, 1958, p. vii.

important either of itself or because of the income and prestige it can bring; in the other, it is only a method of obtaining money to meet felt needs.

The result of this contradiction is to make it possible to introduce into formal economics the insights of Weber and Tawney; they showed that it was the attitude of the population to work and leisure, consumption and saving that determines the rate of growth. This idea was further developed by Walt Rostow in his book *The Process of Economic Growth*. It also underlines the close connection between economics and anthropology, a discipline that has always insisted that different societies will value varied ways of life.

If it is accepted that societies will have different attitudes toward work and leisure, this challenges the validity of existing neoclassical theory, which is based on the assumption that the amount of work people carry out will remain the same even though income increases.

In countries where work is not accepted as good in itself an increase in income will tend to lead to a decrease in hours of work. In these circumstances even the most basic neoclassical economic theorems, such as those relating supply and demand, will be invalidated.

It is impossible to mention here every source from which my analysis has been drawn: like all authors of syntheses I have drawn upon much previous theory. Nevertheless, there are certain major debts I would like to acknowledge. Professor Richard Goodwin taught me to examine economic theory rather than accept it uncritically—I can only hope that he will be satisfied with the results. Dr. F. Pamp, of the American Management Association, Dr. J. Polk and Dr. Audrey Duckert, read early drafts of the manuscript and helped greatly with their comments—some of which I stubbornly refused to accept.

Two further major debts remain; they so often form the conventional ending to a preface that it is difficult to give them the meaning they deserve. First to Mr. Victor Weybright of the New American Library, who took time to consider a manuscript from an unknown author and who could see merit in an early and inadequate draft. Second, to my wife, who has unjustly (but perhaps wisely) refused to be named as joint author.

Part I

THE POOR COUNTRIES

I. *The Present Division:*
Riches and Poverty

THIS IS THE AGE of rapid communication. Every day a bewildering mass of information is presented to us in conversation, by watching television, listening to the radio, or through reading newspapers, magazines, and, occasionally, books. Our familiar world is disrupted by floods of facts about such subjects as new types of raw materials and finished products, innovations in methods and techniques, scientific discoveries, riots or unrest, the emergence of new nations. It is obviously impossible for each person to examine all the implications of every fact; should we, therefore, entirely abandon the struggle to comprehend events and passively rely on the interpretations of specialists in each field? This does not seem a good way out of our dilemma. In the first place a specialist specializes, that is to say he restricts his activities to one area, disclaiming all competence in others. His interpretations are further limited in time and space according to when and where particular events took place. As a result we often find that, when we have added together all the experts' interpretations of a series of events, we possess a wealth of opinions, covering many aspects of the subject in great detail, but lacking concurring features that would enable us to form a coherent picture of the total situation or at least to perceive the outline of a pattern implicit in the events.

In the foreground of the world scene today are events usually discussed under the various headings: "political," "economic," and "social"; these classifications are frequently treated separately by political scientists, economists, and sociologists. The purpose of this book is to discuss an "economic" subject, world economic development—both national and international—against the background of all the social sciences. Social, economic, and political factors will not be treated in separate compartments but as aspects of a whole. As we examine the situation in the poor countries we will find that their stability, and indeed their very existence, depends on rapid economic growth—and that this will normally be attainable only if aid is given to them by other countries. We will also learn that many of these countries are prepared to abandon material benefits if this is necessary to attain apparent freedom from outside control. In the rich countries of the world we will see that for the first time enlightened self-interest and generosity accord. Changing conditions demand that we develop new social attitudes appropriate to the age in which we live; greater assistance will have to be given, not only to the unfortunate within national borders, but also to the poorer countries of the world if global unrest is to be avoided.

Unless we understand why the comments of specialists cannot easily be combined to form a meaningful whole, we cannot set out to build an over-all framework that will allow us to understand the problems of economic development. In his recent book, *The Affluent Society,* Professor Galbraith coined a phrase, "the conventional wisdom." By this he meant that comment is often based on relationships that were once valid but are no longer appropriate in the changed conditions. In his book he concentrated on the inapplicability of ideas and ideals conceived in the nineteenth century to serve as guides in the twentieth. A single example of the tendency to continue to defend and even advocate outmoded ideas will suffice. Capitalism is still suggested as the only proper form of organization for society in the rich countries of the world and proposed for adoption elsewhere, although it has long since been replaced by a modified system more appropriate for the age in which we live. Ralph Cordiner, chairman of General Electric, stated the whole issue succinctly: "Within our own country, the lag between theory and practice is reflected in wasteful frictions and antagonisms between government, business, unions, education and other institutions. Because of the national obsession with concepts that are no longer relevant—concepts of old world capitalism and old world socialism—each of these groups finds much of its own work frustrated or attacked on the basis of wholly obsolete assumptions as to the nature of economic life in the United States today." This tendency, however, is not confined to America; throughout the world ideas, institutions, and ideals develop lives of their own and continue to exist despite the fact that they are no longer appropriate. It is equally vital, however, to remember that the new concepts now developing in the rich countries are often useless or even damaging in the poorer areas of the world.

The second major difficulty in securing an over-all understanding of events results from the artificial barriers created by those studying the behavior of man. Confronted with the growing complexity of knowledge, various academic disciplines specialized in aspects of human behavior. The economist dealt with trade and money-making, the psychologist studied mental processes, the sociologist examined societies, and the anthropologist tried to cover the whole field but concentrated largely on isolated groups—hoping to develop from this study generalized laws.

Economics went furthest in its attempts to limit its discussion to certain characteristics of man. Unfortunately man's nature refused to divide itself to coincide with these distinctions. His motives remain complex—he considers *all* the factors of which he is aware when making a decision. Economic motives are not adequate to explain all economic phenomena, for the amount of attention people attach to money-making depends on the comparative value they place on work and leisure, on consumption and saving. If they find work and high incomes pleasant, they will spend much time on their jobs; if they prefer leisure and have little use for a higher income, other ways of spending their time will appear more important. Nevertheless a very large part of present-day economic analysis is still based on the assumption that man's money-making interests can be isolated—this theory is normally described as neoclassical economics.

Proposals based on this theory are still put forward by economists although their attitudes toward it are curiously ambivalent. When dealing with their own specialty economists often realize that the theory is inadequate and introduce many additional complications. However, when discussing subjects other than their own field of study, they are prone to accept without discussion the conclusions reached on the basis of incomplete assumptions. One of the threads running through this study will, therefore, be a challenge to various theories devised on the basis of neoclassical assumptions.

One of the basic beliefs in this theory is that each man's behavior is unaffected by the society in which he lives. In actual fact peoples' reactions—although they are not *entirely* determined by the countries in which they are brought up —are greatly affected by them. Some cultures attach great importance to work and to the consumption made possible by this work; others attach less or even consider consumption definitely bad. A quotation by an expert on consumption economics, Ruth Mack, develops this idea: " . . . consumption, possessions, purchasing, are matters of highly charged significance to peoples of the Western world and probably especially to North Americans. Some possessions are important in any culture. But money and goods are in ours a central core—in the sense (though not to the extent) that magic ritual to propitiate gods of fertility were central in the life of the Zuni Indians, or warlike prowess and endurance in the Sioux plains culture or loyalty to family and friends in Confucianism."

It is these differences in attitudes that essentially determine whether economic development occurs or fails to take place. The importance given to work and leisure, consumption and saving will determine the rate of growth as Weber and Tawney pointed out in books published many years ago. However, their insights could not be incorporated into neo-classical theory, which assumed that *all* firms tried to gain as large a profit as possible (i.e., "maximise their profits")— once this had been accepted it was illogical to argue that firms in some countries might be more interested in obtaining large profits than those in others. Apart from Joseph Schumpeter's pioneering work, it is only in recent years that such economists as James Duesenberry, Walt Rostow, and W. A. Lewis have tried to reintroduce social factors into economics, and to show that the different attitudes of populations would affect economic development. Growth will occur when the inhabitants of a country are willing to work hard, and also to spend time producing "investment goods" —machines, factories, dams—which will increase the amount of production in future years.

When economic problems are being considered, the world can be divided into two major groups of countries: the developed and the underdeveloped. These terms, however, betray the prejudices of those who coined them, for the difference between these two parts of the world is not in terms of underdevelopment with its pejorative tones of backwardness not only in economics but in social organization: it is quite simply between poverty and riches. These countries will therefore be called the rich and poor countries throughout this work. These must, however, be recognized as "shorthand" terms expressing a very complex reality.

The division between the rich and poor countries is a simple one: incomes in the poor countries are only a fraction of those in the rich. There are now a few exceptions to this statement: the wealth in certain of the oil-rich countries could provide a reasonable standard of living for everyone. But certain characteristics associated with past poverty would still exist. The poor countries have in the past put little stress on the importance of work that would increase the material standard of living, have had a low level of formal education, and have developed a set of traditional values that are deeply embedded in the minds of the people of the country. However, all these characteristics are now changing with increasing speed as these countries become aware of values adopted in other parts of the world. The rich countries are distinguished by defining status largely in terms of business, money, consumption, and saving and by having achieved a relatively high standard of living.

The main economic difference between the two sets of

countries is that in the poor countries social factors will combine to limit the rate of saving and investment—the increase in supply will not keep up with the rising demand for goods. In the rich countries, on the other hand, the increase in the supply of goods tends to be so rapid, because of heavy expenditures in investment, that there are more goods available than people can afford to buy. There is therefore a fundamental difference between the problems of the poor countries, where supply tends to be insufficient, and those of the rich countries, where excess productive capacity has often led to slumps.

While the essential features of the rich and poor countries can be easily defined, no attempt can—or need—be made to draw a rigid line between the two groups. There are countries in all stages of development. Those that would be generally accepted as being rich are in North America, Northern Europe, and Australasia. Almost all the countries in Asia, Africa, the Middle East, and South and Central America would be considered poor, although some observers would argue that certain countries in Latin America should be excluded from this category. The analysis in Africa is sometimes complicated by the existence of multiracial societies. It would be generally agreed that Japan's position is exceptional, for she shares few of the attitudes of the poor countries but is still relatively impoverished. We will see in Chapter XI that her problems stem largely from restrictions on international trade.

Although the economic situation in Russia and Eastern Europe is likely to resemble that of the rich countries in future years, no attempt is made to discuss their problems here because state control makes possible a greatly increased range of policy measures. On the other hand, the problems of the Chinese and the methods available for their solution often resemble those of the other poor countries. Although it is often suggested that Chinese policies are based on communist doctrines, we will find that the steps taken by the government often reflect not ideological beliefs but the harsh compulsion of events, and that other poor countries will have to examine the applicability of these measures to their problems.

Although the division of the world into rich and poor countries is justifiable because of the basic resemblance between the attitudes of the nations within each of these groups, this naturally does not mean that the beliefs of any two poor or rich countries will be identical. The history of each rich and each poor country will have caused them to value different ways of life and to control their societies in varied ways. Although, for example, all the Western powers share a belief in democracy, the ways in which their parliaments are elected, the relationship between the parties, and the degree of party discipline differ. In the poor countries methods of control have often been very different from those of the West, and there can be no certainty that Western democratic patterns will be suitable; each country will have its own problems and solutions. Because of the differences between values policies that would be suitable in one country might have unfavorable results in another; suggestions that would be appropriate to cure a problem in one nation might aggravate it elsewhere.

The existence of over one hundred nations, each with its own system and values, makes it impossible for any person to know the proper policies for each of them. No attempt is made to discover the precise measures suitable for any country here. This book is designed to explore the relationships of events, to demonstrate that the assumptions on which policies are at present based are often inappropriate, and that the steps taken on the basis of false theories worsen rather than improve the situation. We will see that the attainment of economic growth cannot usually be ensured by "economic actions" but requires the existence of certain social attitudes to work and leisure, consumption and saving, investment and innovation.

The problems of the relationships between the rich and poor countries are often discussed in terms of the cold war, of the moves necessary to ensure that countries remain committed to one side or the other. This approach is not adopted here for two reasons. First, because it is believed that the problems of the poor countries are not susceptible to analysis in terms of communism and capitalism; these areas face a problem unique in human history and it is only if the situation is considered without preconceptions that a solution will be possible. The second reason for avoiding this approach is that the cold war has become an anachronism in the age of the hydrogen bomb; either the world survives together or it will blow itself to pieces. The poor countries cannot be treated as pawns in a power struggle; aid must be given to a country, not to buttress one side or the other in an ideological struggle, but to help the inhabitants.

One final warning. The whole analysis of the book is based on the present situation; its relevance is conditional on the continuing validity of the description of conditions in the poor and rich countries. When changes take place— as they will during coming years—the analysis will become inaccurate and the solutions inappropriate. The social sciences can never be an exact discipline, for the conditions they examine are constantly changing.

The book has three parts: a discussion of the poor countries, of the rich countries, and of the relationships between them. Although it is designed to be read in the order in which it is written, each of the three sections can be studied independently. We will find that the problems of the poor countries are almost insoluble without help from the rich;

however, because of the limited volume of aid at the present
time and in order to present the argument as simply as
possible, the implications of aid are set out in the last section of the book rather than scattered among the chapters
on the rich and poor countries.

II. *Tradition and Change*

THE AMOUNT OF attention devoted to the problems of the poor countries has increased rapidily in the years since the Second World War; analysis has concentrated on the poverty of these areas and the need to raise the standard of living. Many observers, in emphasizing the urgency of economic growth, have failed to understand that this is not the most difficult task facing the poor countries. Their main problem is to adjust present beliefs to modern world conditions at a sufficiently rapid rate to prevent the breakdown of their societies.

At the present time the poor countries have conceptions and beliefs very different from those of the West. The value-systems in which they are embodied have regulated lives for many centuries and are therefore unquestioned except by the modern generation, which is now exercising increasing influence. Some of the value-systems of these countries are undoubtedly weak in those areas the West has come to accept as most important, but they usually have their own strengths, most notably a joy in living that cannot always be found among the material plenty of the rich countries. One of the most difficult lessons to learn is that ways of life that are alien to one's own can be vital and satisfying—that it is not necessarily wise to try to introduce the values of one's own society to others. The easiest way to gain this insight is perhaps by observant travel, but for those who have not had this opportunity the realization can come through reading. In the bibliography at the end of this book are listed a few outstanding treatments of societies that help to demonstrate this point.

The distrust, and sometimes distaste, with which those from the rich countries regard the values of the poor is partially due to the fact that many members of the poor countries believe that the world is not entirely governed by the logical rules of science, but that supernatural actions can affect events. It would not be appropriate to examine the evidence for and against these attitudes here. One cannot fail, however, to be impressed by the way in which individuals from Western countries who have approached these matters with open or skeptical minds have come away with their convictions about magic considerably altered or even reversed. Nor does it appear sensible to shrug off the evidence amassed by scientific studies of such matters as extrasensory perception. It is also useful to remember that science itself is coming to admit that its descriptions of reality are subjective.

Much of the unfavorable comment on the behavior of populations in the poor countries has been based on the conduct of individuals who have been demoralized by long absence from their tribe or village, and forced by conditions in the towns to base their actions on unrestricted self-interest, giving free rein to their emotions and abandoning the tribal ethics that made primitive life humane. J. C. Carothers makes this point clearly; he refers to Africa, but his views have wider application: "Life in Africa was highly insecure; but the individual did achieve some inner sense of personal security by adherence, and only by adherence, to the traditional rules—rules which received their sanction and much of their force from the "will" of ancestors whose spirits were conceived as powerful and as maintaining their attachment to the land. There were fears, of course, and misfortunes were almost the order of the day, but even these were seldom without precedent and for each there were pre-scribed behaviour patterns, which satisfied the urge to action, so that the African achieved a measure of stability and, within his group and while at home, was courteous, usually self-sufficient and, in effect, a social being."

The social changes that destroyed the hold of traditional values have also revolutionized many of the desires and atti-tudes of the populations of the poor countries. They have realized that it is possible to live longer and in a better state of health, and they are therefore unwilling to do without medical treatment; they have appreciated that it is possible to have a higher standard of living and they intend to obtain it. The possibility of meeting these new demands will be greatly influenced by the fact that a very large proportion of the citizens of these countries live in rural areas and are engaged in agriculture. It is estimated that about 70 per cent of the Indian population is engaged in agriculture and forestry, hunting and fishing, and the proportions are similar in other poor countries—only about 12 per cent of the labor force was in these occupations in the United States in 1950.

Agriculturalists are often particularly difficult to convince of the value of change, for they have lived with their land for many years and their ancestors have passed down their accumulated wisdom to them—they believe they *know* the ways of obtaining the largest possible crops. In addition, since so many live on the margin of poverty, the risk of failure of an experiment must be expected to bulk large in their calculations. They may well consider it better to continue to obtain a small but certain return, rather than adopt new techniques that have apparently led to larger crops on nearby land belonging to someone else. This resistance to change is sometimes increased by the fact that their culture explains success in growing crops in terms of magic, luck, or other non-scientific reasons.

The individuals who have attempted to introduce changes that would improve the position have often unwittingly increased their own difficulties by examining neither the way in which the society was organized nor its aims. A failure to adopt an innovation has then been described as showing the stupidity of people, whereas it normally only illustrated the fact that the proposed change was either inappropriate to the society's needs or that it had been badly presented. An individual will always adopt a change if he believes that it will increase his satisfaction. One illustration of this lack of understanding followed the failure of certain Middle Eastern villages to adopt piped water—such an innovation appeared highly favorable to those attempting to introduce it, since it would eliminate the need to carry water from the wells, which were sometimes located at a considerable distance from the village. But this proposal was often rejected because the time women spent at the well provided an opportunity for valued conversation—their only recreation.

Another interesting example resulted from the introduction of improved wheat seed in India. Within one village the new seed was sown by two or three farmers, but they abandoned its use after a couple of seasons although they admitted that its yield was considerably higher. Such an action appears incomprehensible, but an observer who lived in the village found that the decision was the result of rational calculation. The improved seed was made available on credit, but one condition of borrowing was that the same amount of seed should be returned immediately after the harvest in pure condition—thus the farmer had no possibility of guarding against a poor wheat year by mixing other flour grains with the wheat when sowing, as was customary. The grains of wheat were found to be too large to be ground with the usual equipment. The dough appeared to the villagers to be harder to bake, while the straw was not suitable for fodder and would not even burn—this deprived farmers of certain additional uses of the older wheat straw. Finally, the bread was considered less tasty.

Failure to realize that decisions are normally made on rational grounds and that unwillingness to adopt a change suggests that it is not suitable for the society has often prejudiced attempts to introduce new methods. Indeed, in some cases the effect of well-meant but imposed innovations in agricultural techniques has been so serious that whole districts were gravely damaged as food-producing areas. In certain parts of Burma, for example, the introduction of the deep plow destroyed the hard layer of earth that held the water in the rice fields. In East Africa the plowing of large tracts of forest land for the ill-fated British peanut scheme is believed to have totally destroyed the soil in many areas, for it is now the consistency of brick and impossible to work.

The result of an innovation is often quite different from that anticipated. In Africa the introduction of industry increased the possibility of earning money and added to economic welfare, but it also disrupted the whole pattern of society. The absence of men from the villages for long periods upset the balance of labor in the tribe. The accepted methods of passing on the traditional values of the society were damaged by the absence of the men; this led to a demoralization that caused the women to move to the towns, where they were often unable to find work.

The last example also illustrates that apparently limited changes in the way of life may alter many more actions than would be anticipated by casual examination. This was also demonstrated in a striking way by the events that followed the first purchase of a wagon by a group of Papago Indians in Southern Arizona. Previously they had not used wheeled transport but had moved about on horseback. It was clear that the innovation would have extensive results. While some were predicted by the agent of the United States Bureau of Indian Affairs, others surprised him. Indeed the very pattern of use would not have been anticipated—the wagon was not treated as private property but like a unique resource, the land, which had to be fairly shared by all the members of the community.

The introduction of the wagon made it necessary to develop new skills and rendered obsolete other attainments that had previously been vital. The manufacture of panniers and pack saddles for horses was abandoned, and since pottery was found too fragile for transportation by wagon, its manufacture was greatly curtailed. Metal barrels took its place. On the other hand, individuals learned to work metal in order to shoe horses and also to repair the metal rims on wagon wheels. Changes took place in the utilization of time; before the introduction of the wagon, wood was collected in small quantities and at frequent intervals by women and children; afterward it became worth while occasionally to send out parties of men to cut wood and take it to market. This additional source of money was used to pay for the manufactured harness, metal wagon parts and barrels that had become necessary to the Papago. Thus the introduction of one wagon led to changes in many areas of life and the impact was further increased at a later date when the village came to own several wagons and other new equipment.

A report, "Cultural Patterns and Technical Change," published by the United Nations Educational, Cultural and Scientific Organization (UNESCO) examined the effects of changes in social organization and suggested that, if new developments take place too rapidly and are of too radical a nature, the society may break down and the individual be left without any support, developing mental or bodily sickness, or becoming apathetic to events. It suggested five major types of reactions that can occur when tensions caused by change become too acute. First, people may return to old forms of behavior, which will now appear less satisfactory because of new knowledge. Second, behavior may become less mature, more childish and irresponsible. Third, the accumulated tensions from frustration or difficulties of adjustment may find relief in aggressive acts that need not be connected with the individual or situation that originally caused the tension. Fourth, the individual may withdraw physically or psychologically from the frustrating situation; such withdrawal may be into apathy or substitute activities such as alcoholism. Fifth, individuals may resort to prevention or partial prevention of tensions by manifesting feelings of chronic fatigue or by assigning blame for the unfortunate situation to others. Such a list of possible reactions is naturally not exhaustive, but it may help to explain why attempts to aid the development of societies have often led to unexpected results that proved difficult to explain or resolve.

What are the causes of these reactions? In the poor countries where the rate of change in the past has typically been slow, any alteration is potentially more disruptive than in the fast-changing rich countries. The populations of the poor countries have used the same objects and techniques for centuries. The role of one object is often interwoven with that of another, with the customs of the society, and with the supernatural beings believed to be responsible for the use of the object and the welfare and safety of the people.

For example, the culture of most Australian aboriginal tribes was based on the concept that their society was originally established by "mildly marvellous ancestral beings." Their life was organized so as to approach this original state as closely as possible. The arrival of missionaries deprived the aborigines of complete control over their lives, for the missionaries were not responsible to the tribal authorities and felt free to introduce elements of Western culture. New goods were distributed. This attacked the whole value-system of the tribe and also the relationships fundamental to its social organization.

The way in which values were undermined can perhaps best be illustrated by the events following the replacement of stone axes by steel axes. The stone ax had been the traditional work implement of the tribe, it was an outward sign of the importance of the male as well as a mark of seniority. No woman could own an ax; she had to borrow one, normally from her husband or father. As the most important tool, it also played a part in trading relationships and feasts. The missionaries made no allowance for these factors and distributed the more efficient steel axes indiscriminately to men and women, old or young; the female recipients regarded the new axes as their own, although within the value-system of the tribe they had been unable to "own" the stone ax. An old man, who would previously always have been respectfully asked to lend his ax, was often forced to recognize the greater efficiency of the steel ax, by borrowing one from a younger man or even a woman; concepts of status and prestige became completely confused. In addition, feasts that were held largely to acquire ax heads lost their main purpose and were infrequently held. At the time the study of the tribe was made these and other changes were leading to complete social breakdown. In other areas where contact with the white man had been more extensive ". . . native behaviour and native sentiments are simply dead. Apathy reigns. The aboriginal has passed beyond the reach of any outsider who might wish to do him well or ill."

The life of the Australian aborigine was destroyed by contact with a civilization he did not understand and that the new settlers insisted he should adopt. An equally grave danger results when the poor countries try to employ ideas developed in the rich countries without examining whether they will be appropriate in the different set of conditions of the poor. For example, labor unions have often assumed that because their main task in the rich countries is to increase wages, their role in the poor ones *must* be the same. Wage increases, however, may be ineffective in reducing tensions and may even increase them, as is shown by a recent study of the labor force of a United Fruit factory in Tiquisate, Guatemala. Continuous labor-management bargaining had pushed wages up to a level three or four times as high as those of agricultural workers who carried out approximately the same amount of work. Tensions did not develop between factory workers and agriculturalists over wage differentials, as might have been expected on the basis of Western experience, but among the factory workers themselves. There was no socially accepted way of spending high earnings. It was, in effect, the attempt to get rid of the available money that caused tensions.

Some money was sent away to friends and relatives who were less well off—this was a generally accepted form of social behavior. Part of it was spent in an attempt to obtain a higher standard of living by the purchase of radios, watches, etc. But a substantial amount was spent on alcohol; consumption being very large not only in actual quantity but also in comparison with the accepted drinking habits of the area. There was an increase in prostitution, considerable family desertion, irregularity in social relations and a sharp diminution of community spirit. The factory workers had real grievances; there was a lack of privacy and no opportunity for the expression of individual interests such as the planting of gardens. All resentments, however, were channeled into the accepted pattern of protest—a demand for more money. Hoping to restore good relations, the management would agree to raise wages; more money would then be available and this would further aggravate the situation.

A sudden demand for paid labor has often led to temporary situations of this sort as wages rise and the desire for consumption goods does not develop as rapidly. A more serious problem, however, is that there is little comprehension in many of the poor countries that the increasingly general desire for a higher standard of living can only be satisfied if the population is willing to work hard and if investment is carried out. In the former colonial possessions the process of securing independence from foreign governments was often identified with the beginning of a golden age in which want and suffering would be abolished. The nationalist leaders claimed that the colonial power had prevented the fair distribution of the natural wealth of the country and had profited by sending its abundance of raw materials to the home country. Such reasoning was, of course, popular in itself as part of the criticism of a disliked government, but it also seemed logical. Foreigners from the rich country had a visibly high standard of living, obtained for work that appeared to be less arduous than that of the inhabitants of the country. There was naturally little understanding of the work and sacrifice that had been necessary in the past to build this standard of living, or knowledge of the continuing laborious daily round carried out by the majority of the "foreigners" in their home country. Their wealth appeared inexplicable, unless it was being achieved by using the resources of the country in which they held positions of authority.

For many only one further step was necessary to conclude that the success of the foreigner was obtained by supernatural means. In many areas of the world the accepted reason for good and bad crops is the relative strength of one's magic or the power of one's gods. The success of foreigners is therefore attributed to the help of *their* gods and what could be more logical in these circumstances than to petition one's own, requesting the goods that the rich countries seemed to have in such abundance? It is this reaction that has led to what is often described as cargo cults, magico-religious groups found over a wide area of the Pacific. Believers await the arrival of vast quantities of the types of goods they have seen in the possession of foreigners, and that will be sent them by the usual modern methods of transport, ship or plane. Warehouses are built, quays and airstrips are constructed. In some cases crops have even been destroyed so the inhabitants can plead their real poverty before a god who has been slow to provide them with the necessities of modern life they too deserve.

People can act sensibly only when they feel that they understand and control their surroundings; if they do not, they will cease to be aware of their best interests—and reactions similar to those described will result. Economic growth is a necessary goal for the poor countries, but it must not be considered to outweigh all others, nor should it be assumed that every action that increases wealth is necessarily right. Economic development will only be satisfactory if it acts to preserve the meaning of life, not to destroy it.

The cost of development in the rich countries of the world was tragically high, and already in the poor countries too many people have been torn from their environment and left with no ties that could enable them to orient their lives. The minimum amount of change required to enable the poor countries to achieve the economic growth that is vital will be so great as to lead to widespread mental stress. Every effort must be made to avoid unnecessary alterations in the existing pattern of life, to strip innovations of all accretions that could complicate their adoption, to realize that institutions are only means to reach given ends and not ends in themselves. Even if these precautions were fully adopted, irreparable damage to the lives of many human beings will be unavoidable, for they will be unable to understand and therefore control their situations.

The introduction of change in the poor countries, and particularly innovations associated with economic development, often involves contact between people from a predominantly industrial culture and societies that are closer to nature and attach less importance to goods. The person who attempts to introduce innovations brings with him, not only technical information in his own field, but also a set of deeply rooted ideals about the utility of economic growth and the benefits of a higher standard of living. Consciously, he is often hardly aware of them or of the fact that they cut across the whole value-system of the country in which he is working. If the benefit that the foreigner brings through increasing production is not to be offset by damage to the individual and society, it is essential that his beliefs should affect his technical advice as little as possible and that he should be willing to compromise. The success of his mission cannot be measured only by the rise in production that results; the effect on non-economic areas of life must also be examined—only too often this latter factor is ignored because it cannot be accurately measured.

The present culture of the poor countries is altered not only by members of the rich countries. When men from the poor countries come into contact with the rich, they sometimes repudiate their heritage and adopt all the ideas and ideals of the rich country. Such people have often proved fanatical about destroying the "outdated" values of their own society, as was shown by a recent talk given by an Indian over the air from the British Broadcasting Corporation in London. He blamed the British for not having interfered with the religious convictions of the Hindus and Mohammedans during the period of colonial rule in India. He suggested that the continuation of Hindu and Mohammedan laws was wrong if they conflicted in any way with the moral views of Western countries. For him civilization had become equated with the values existing in the West.

The UNESCO publication already mentioned, which deals with the implications of too rapid technological change, suggests reasons why many who come into contact with the West will insist that all its values are better than those of the country in which they were born, ". . . . a great many of those who acquire an education in medicine, or engineering, or agriculture, will have had to make a considerable break with their own traditions, and will have compensated for this by embracing—with the self-protective zeal and blindness of the convert—the beliefs and practices which they associate with the new knowledge. Their willingness to assume a whole series of symbols—from fountain pens, raincoats and briefcases to an insistence upon marriage for love and the disregard of traditional patterns of inter-personal relations—is often an essential step in the particular path of modernization or Westernization on which they have determined, or for which their own society has selected them." For this same reason it is argued that they are not the most suitable people to introduce change in areas that are still tightly controlled by their traditional cultures.

The social problems of the poor countries of the world—the need to change their beliefs, in order to bring them into accord with modern conditions, coupled with the danger of too rapid alterations—will form a background to the discussion in following chapters of the ways to achieve the economic growth that is vital if increasing populations are to be fed and clothed and rising tastes to be satisfied. We must bear in mind that economic growth is not good in itself, but only in so far as it helps to solve the problems and increase the meaning of the life of each man, woman, and child.

III. *Rising Expectations*

A FEW YEARS AGO the change in the poor countries was dramatized in the phrase "a revolution of rising expectations." It was argued that the populations of these countries will not be satisfied unless their standard of living rises more rapidly in the future; that unless their poverty is alleviated, serious unrest would inevitably occur. Discussion of the problems raised by these assertions must start with an examination of the present difference in standards of living of the rich and poor countries.

Unfortunately there is no satisfactory way to make such a calculation. Conventional figures show that the yearly income per head of some two thirds of the world's population is below $150, while the before-tax income of the United States averages around $2500, and that of much of Europe around $1000. If these figures were accurate, it would seem that living conditions in the poor countries must be impossibly grinding. However, they are calculated in such a way as to overstate the difference between the incomes of the poor and rich countries. For example, the money value of domestic work performed by wives is excluded from income, and these services form a far larger *proportion* of the total value of goods and services in the poor countries than in the rich. In addition, some part of the income of the population of the rich countries is spent so that money can be earned, for example in commuting to and from work. In order to contrast the incomes of various countries, the national currency is converted into dollars but at rates that do not usually reflect the real cost of goods. For all these reasons the currency of the poor countries will actually buy more than is suggested by this comparison—an individual in a poor country with an income calculated by these conventions to be worth $100 will actually be able to attain as high a standard of living as he would have in the United States with an income of, say, $500. Another comparison is sometimes used and this is more adequate; the amount of work required to buy certain types of goods. Although this still overstates the difference, it is certainly more accurate.

The overstatement of the difference in wealth between the rich and poor countries has increased the apparent difficulties of the latter—the process of catching up with the rich countries is made to appear even more impossible than it actually is. The psychological effect of this overstatement is greatly enhanced by the fact that the West has come to look on the level of income as an index of welfare. This definition of welfare tends to assume that work and consumption are the highest goals in life. However, the importance attached to a higher material standard of living is a relatively new development. In earlier centuries wants were stable even in the West and this led to widespread complaints, for example in England, that the result of giving workers higher wages was not a better but an inferior quality of industry, not more but less labor. As needs could be satisfied with a shorter period at work, many skilled laborers who were able to earn as much money as they required in less than the conventional work week spent only three or four days at their jobs and the rest in idleness. The generalized desire for more goods and therefore a higher income and the increasingly accepted demand for a disciplined labor force have lessened the frequency of this type of reaction in the West in the twentieth century.

In the poor countries, the desire for a higher standard of living developed at a later date and, indeed, is only now growing in many areas. In Burma at the turn of the century, rice fields were often left unharvested after the wants of the farmer has been satisfied, despite the existence of markets in which the grain could have been sold. The recruitment of a labor force for a textile factory in the middle of a poor agricultural district in Guatemala proceeded with great difficulty, although the wages offered by the factory were substantially higher than those in agriculture—it took fifty years to build a relatively stable labor force. In Indonesia before the Second World War, a rise in wages commonly caused a decrease in the number of hours the labor force worked; it was now possible to satisfy the desire for goods with less expenditure of time. The effect in some cases was so marked that it proved necessary to cancel the wage increase, which had reduced the available supply of labor rather than increased it. The same reaction has been observed throughout the poorer countries of the world and particularly in the Pacific, where during the war the United States Army introduced American ideas about pay scales onto islands that had been accustomed to wages at a fraction of this level or even to areas where wage payment was unknown.

Further evidence of the relative unimportance of an abundance of goods in certain areas is provided by a series of essays written about 1950 by twenty-six children in Guatemala and twenty-six in Iowa, U.S.A., on the subject: "My Home, What I Like about It, What I Do Not Like, My Ambitions for My Home in the Future." These showed that the ideals of the children in these two different countries varied widely. Twenty-two of the twenty-six children from Iowa mentioned the importance of material facilities and none of those from Guatemala; twenty-three out of twenty-six from Guatemala mentioned love and peace in the home as compared to thirteen in the U.S.A., and eighteen from Guatemala mentioned the importance of space as compared to three in the U.S.A.

The pressure of increasing wants is now moving into all areas of the world. It has been brought about by increasing contact of members of the poor countries with the continually rising standards of the rich, which are dramatized by the circulation abroad of Hollywood films and glossy magazines, and by the travel of businessmen and tourists from the rich countries. Wants have been further increased by the realization that lives can be prolonged and education made available to all and in some cases by exaggerated hopes that were raised by nationalist leaders as they attempted to gain their freedom from occupying powers or in their attempt to win elections.

This increasing desire for a higher standard of living has not always been associated with a willingness to accept hard work and saving, which are necessary if economic growth is to be attained. Indeed, the contrary tendency is often observed, for any increase in wants for consumption goods tends to reduce the amount of saving carried out and therefore the amount of money that is available for investment. For if income remains unchanged while the amount of goods people want to buy increases, they will feel less willing to save. Rises in income must accompany increasing tastes if a decrease in the amount of money available for investment —and therefore a fall in the rate of economic growth—is not to result.

Several other values and beliefs current in the poor countries tend to decrease the amount of money people are willing and able to put aside from their income and make available for productive investment. In most of these countries, success has traditionally been dramatized both in the richer and the poorer classes by "conspicuous consumption." Gold and silver, houses and land have been some of the ways in which wealth has been stored, and any attempt to encourage people to keep their savings in monetary form meets strong resistance, which is increased at the present time by rapid inflation in many of these countries.

The values of many of the poor countries demand that each man should be responsible for the support of all his kindred, who may be very numerous because individuals are often considered to be closely related to an extended family or indeed to a whole tribe. The increase in the number of people who will demand support if additional income is obtained has discouraged many from undertaking additional work. This provides a good illustration of the complexities that confront those attempting to encourage economic growth. The destruction of family ties as well as tribal or caste cohesion would appear, at first sight, to be a method of increasing the rate of growth, for it would tend to augment the amount of work done. Even on a strictly economic level, however, this reasoning is incomplete. The destruction of this private system of aid would make it essential for the state to provide for those who became destitute—a burden few poor countries would wish to meet at the present time as a large part of the population is either unemployed or, where work is available only some of the time, underemployed. If the sums necessary for the state to undertake this task could be raised, it would be only by large increases in taxes, and the effect of this step on the amount of work carried out would be very severe. From a social point of view, it is difficult to contemplate with equanimity the effect on the society and the individual of the complete and rapid destruction of traditional family ties, however limiting or burdensome they may sometimes be.

Perhaps the most important bar to increasing savings and investments is the one that has applied throughout the ages and that was first systematically examined by Malthus —the pressure of increasing population. In most poor countries there is still a direct relationship between the amount of food available and the number of children who survive—infant mortality depends very heavily on the ability of the mother and child to obtain an adequate diet. A larger food supply often leads to an immediate increase in the number of people who must be fed and thus cannot be used to increase the standard of living.

In postwar years major efforts have been made to reduce the toll of disease and to lengthen life expectancies — as a result, the rise in the amount of food available has sometimes lagged behind the increase in population. Population growth throughout the poor countries is now at an average rate of well over 1 per cent per year and in many areas exceeds 2 and even 3 per cent. Unless birth rates fall to levels that can be brought about only through a world-wide adoption of the practice of contraception, it is expected that the population of the world will double in the next thirty years, rising from 2.7 billion to 5.4 billion.

It is often suggested that any effort to reduce birth rates would run into almost insuperable difficulties, and there are many who claim that parents in these countries are so accustomed to large families that they would be unwilling to consider limiting their number of children. However, whenever serious studies of attitudes have been made, a large proportion of the population has accepted the need to reduce family size. The need for a reduction in births is so urgent and obvious that even the moral stigma attached to birth control by certain religious organizations or other groups is not sufficient to prevent couples from being willing to practice it.

A study of the probable effects of different levels of the birth rate on the economic development of India illustrates the importance of this problem. Three sets of figures were developed on the basis of different assumptions about the future birth rate; in the first it was assumed that the number of live births would decline immediately and continue down to half its present level by 1981; in the second that there would be no change in the birth rate until 1966 and then a decline so steep that the rate would be cut in half by 1981; the third model assumes that the rate would remain at its present level till 1986. In the first case it is estimated that income per head would practically double by 1986, in the second that it would rise by about two thirds, and in the third that the rise would only be about one third. It is not suggested by the authors of this survey that these calculations represent anything more than projections based on necessarily uncertain hypotheses; they are cited here because they show the importance of birth rates in determining the rate of increase in income per head. Indeed, some authorities are far more pessimistic and suggest that unless a decrease in the birth rate can be obtained in the near future there will be a *fall* in the standard of living. The situation in some areas of the world is even more serious; populations are larger than can be supported by the available natural resources.

In many of the poor countries there is already a shortage of workable agricultural land. As children grow up they are unable to find any form of work in their village or district; there is no land available for purchase or on which they can labor for others. The only prospect of self-support is by working in industry, which is largely concentrated in the towns. Even when there is no shortage of agricultural land and no difficulty in finding work in the countryside, there is still a movement toward the towns in many poor countries, for people consider that they have a better chance of obtaining a satisfactory standard of living there. Unfortunately, only too often they are forced on their arrival into slums that are as bad as, if not worse than, any that existed in Europe or America during the Industrial Revolution. Those who move into the urban areas rarely have the necessary information before they leave with which to make a balanced decision, and those who have already arrived in the towns will often send back word of economic success and better conditions for the sake of their own prestige—even if they have failed to secure a job or reasonable housing.

Only by keeping these facts in mind can one understand the often-condemned measure of the Chinese Government that prevents people from moving into the towns without a permit—whether it will be condoned depends upon personal values. Is it better to keep the peasant in the village against his will or let him move into the towns where he will often be unable to find either a job or a decent place to live? Those who doubt the dangers of the second course or who believe that there should be no difficulty in producing sufficient housing, will find food for thought in a recent United Nations social survey, which describes the multitude of problems faced by the poor countries in keeping up with the urban growth.

The poor countries must find work for the rising population in order to avoid an increase in unemployment. In modern conditions this will almost always require some development of industry. But only people with a relatively rare combination of talents—an ability to distinguish an investment that it is thought will be profitable, coupled with a willingness to take risks—will be able to do this type of work, and the number of these individuals, often called "entrepreneurs," is limited.

The rich countries developed because a large proportion of those capable of acting as entrepreneurs spent their lives endeavoring to increase production regardless of the level their income might reach—their work was quite literally their life. But in the poor countries, business for many is only a way to earn the money necessary for life, and therefore a high income will often lead to a decrease in the amount of effort put forward. Neither will the entrepreneur normally be willing to return a large proportion of his profits to the business in order to promote a rapid rate of growth; he will often prefer to use such funds for investment in real estate or to purchase goods to demonstrate status. Thus one of the major ways in which funds for investment were secured in the early days of economic development in the rich countries is greatly reduced in importance.

The amount of effort and the amount of investment in the poor countries is further limited by two attitudes that originally developed in the rich countries but are now generally adopted in the poor. In the early days of industrialization, entrepreneurs were free to pay low wages and to gain high profits. These could be reinvested to promote economic growth. At the present time, unions insist on wages that keep profits down to a "reasonable" level. This is satisfactory from a humanitarian point of view, but economic growth requires investment; these comparatively high wages reduce the amount of money available for investment; the sums paid to workers in the poor countries are spent on consumption goods and not made available for investment. The second limitation on growth results from the high level of taxation adopted in the poor countries, particularly severe for the highest incomes. Many people therefore feel work is less worth while. This level of taxes also decreases the amount of personal saving carried out and sometimes even encourages those most severely affected to use funds previously saved, in order to maintain their standard of living.

The process of industrialization in the poor countries therefore tends to be slow; the people best able to carry out investments are relatively uninterested in doing so. Since there is little investment, only a relatively small number of new jobs are created, and the increase is inadequate to absorb the rise in the labor force following the growth in population. In addition, because of the distorted price structure of these countries, there is a tendency for too much money to be spent on replacing workers with machinery, thus further aggravating the problem of unemployment.

Many of the poor countries suffer from both unemployment and underemployment. In certain countries this problem is serious only in the urban areas, to which people have moved but where they have been unable to find work. Surveys have shown that in some urban areas in Africa only one person in three or four actually has a job. In other countries where there is a shortage of arable land, unemployment and underemployment are also found in the rural areas.

The rate of development in the poor countries is often insufficiently rapid to keep pace with the increasing population, its growing demand for food, clothing, and Western-type consumption goods. With the present attitudes of the population, decisions of individuals will not cause sufficient economic growth and the government will therefore have to intervene to encourage those actions that will result in increases in production as well as counteract the distortions in productive activity resulting from the present price structure. These problems are taken up in the next chapter.

IV. *Rural vs. Urban —*
the Role of Government

Economic development in the nineteenth century took
place under the influence of one of the most comfortable doctrines ever proposed by man — that the highest
possible level of welfare in society would be achieved if each
person followed his own selfish economic interests and dis-
regarded the effects of his actions on the rest of society.
This idea stemmed from Adam Smith's book, written in
1776, *An Enquiry into the Nature and Causes of the Wealth
of Nations*. Economists devoted much time to the refinement
of this idea during the nineteenth century and by the beginning of the twentieth it was possible to prove, *given
certain assumptions,* that government intervention in the
economy would decrease total welfare.

However, while this doctrine was being developed and
elaborated by economists, changes in political and social
theory were rapidly challenging its validity. The published

findings of various royal commissions in England about the conditions under which women and children labored in the first half of the nineteenth century stirred the public conscience and caused labor acts to be passed; as it was in England that the Industrial Revolution had got under way in the second half of the eighteenth century, so it was also in this country that all the abuses and social misery of unchecked, free competition first became apparent. But as industrialization spread to other countries, the same patterns of exploitation of labor to obtain the maximum profits were observed so long as governments adhered to their policies of non-interference, or "laissez-faire." This led to general agreement that industrialization must be accompanied by some form of government control of competition and conditions of work if the welfare of society were to be ensured.

How, we may ask, was it possible for two such different theories to exist and develop when they were essentially contradictory? Economics held that interference with free competition would act to limit the growth of production and of social welfare, while political theory came to argue that it was the duty of the state to intervene in the economy. The contradiction stemmed from the fact that economic theory had developed in such a way as to isolate itself from the real world and the developments taking place in it. It was indeed true, *given certain assumptions,* that it would be unwise for the state to intervene in the economy, but their validity has been destroyed by the process of industrialization and by changes in social attitudes.

What are these assumptions? They are that: labor is unable to bargain collectively for higher wages; all firms are small; each firm concentrates solely on gaining the largest possible profits; the methods enterprises adopt to obtain their profits will not lessen the welfare of society; firms possess all the information required to carry out efficient production; government does not intervene in the economy in any way. All these assumptions must be realistic if it is to be possible to "prove" that free competition will necessarily maximize the economic welfare of a country.

While many of these assumptions now appear outdated and even ridiculous, this is largely because economic and social conditions throughout the world have changed. However, the result of these alterations is that it is no longer possible to "assume" that government intervention will always be bad; each case must now be treated on its merits. In examining the circumstances that may justify economic intervention by the government, it is convenient to begin by discussing the factors that affect the monetary costs of an action by a firm or person; then to examine the more complicated problem of how the economic actions of a firm may affect the welfare of the country in which it is located; and finally to discuss the long-range problem of how changes in economic structure may affect the values of a nation.

By concentrating their attention on the motives of the individual, economists were able to produce the theory that each person, following his own selfish interests, would serve the goals of society. It was argued that a person confronted with an economic decision would always choose the course of action that would maximize his profits—he would produce at the lowest possible cost and sell at the highest possible price. This would allow more goods to be produced at the same cost or the same amount of goods to be produced at a lower cost—the society would therefore be able to obtain a larger amount of goods. This increase in the amount of production was assumed to result in an automatic rise in the welfare of society.

Exceptions to this rule were recognized at an early date, but it was generally assumed that they were not sufficiently important to destroy the over-all argument. It was understood that certain actions by firms could have an unfavorable effect on the community as a whole despite the increase in profits that resulted for the enterprise. One of the traditional examples has been the firm that allows excessive smoke to escape from its smokestacks; this will normally be relatively costless for the firm in the absence of government penalties, while the introduction of machinery to stop smoke and grit escaping would require expenditure and therefore result in a reduction of profits. On the other hand, the cost to the community of the escaping smoke in additional cleaning of clothes and furnishings and in corrosion caused would normally be far larger than the cost of installing the necessary preventive equipment in the factory. However, cleaning costs do not affect factory profits but are paid for by each member of the community, who cannot normally claim damages from the factory responsible.

The importance of this type of difference between the costs to the firm and those of the community or country as a whole is overshadowed by those caused by unemployment and underemployment. When a firm examines the possibility of installing a new machine or building a factory, it is concerned with the increase in profits that will result. If the change involves a decrease in its labor force, this will reduce the wage bill and therefore be favorable from the point of view of the firm. But it is not certain that this step will be beneficial to the country as a whole. The people displaced by the more efficient techniques, which require fewer employees, may not be able to find a new job, as there are already unemployed workers. Instead of contributing something to the economy as they did when employed, they will produce nothing and be forced to rely on their friends or relations or the government for their support.

The fact that prices of goods, capital, and foreign exchange do not reflect their real value makes calculation of

changes in the total income (national income) of these countries hazardous; this is true, for example, when urban growth
takes place. When people decide to leave their village homes
for the towns, they do so in the hope that they will be more
satisfied there, for unless this were true they would not
move. However, only too often they are unable to find any
form of work and do not add to the amount of goods produced in the economy, while they still require food, clothing,
and shelter. Houses must be built for them if the growth
of slums is to be avoided, and the authorities will sometimes be forced to provide their minimum subsistence needs.
Thus, the movement of people causes immediate costs without any necessary increase in total production.

Those who succeed in obtaining jobs in the city will
normally receive a higher wage than they would have got
in the rural areas; this increase in income will be reflected
in higher national income and is often assumed by economists to imply a higher level of national welfare. But much
of a man's extra income will be spent in purchasing goods
and services he did not require in the past or for which he
paid far less. The space in which he sleeps will often be
extremely high-priced but would hardly have been valued
in the village from which he came. The cost of the meals he
purchases will include the wages of the person cooking the
food; when his mother or wife prepared his meals this was
not calculated as part of income. In addition, the price
paid for food is increased by the cost of transport necessary
to bring it to the towns. The higher incomes people receive
are therefore in large part a recognition of the fact that they
have to pay more in the towns to obtain the same standard
of living—real income has remained almost the same—the
increase is statistical rather than actual.

We can summarize by saying that actions by firms based
on the prices they pay for goods and the level of wages will

not necessarily increase the welfare of society. The economists' claim that they would do so is based on neoclassical economic assumptions. There is, therefore, considerable scope for economists to seek methods of closing the gap between private and social advantage so the actions that the firm finds profitable will also be satisfactory for society. Legislation will often be required, legislation that must not copy that of the rich countries, which do not face the same problem of chronic unemployment.

One of the major policy issues in the poor countries has often been dramatized in terms of the opposing claims of agriculture and industry. Which should be developed? There is really no such dilemma, for it would be impossible in most poor countries to provide sufficient jobs without industrialization, and it would be equally impossible to feed all the population without an increase in agricultural productivity. The true problem does not lie in such simple dichotomies. However, while increases in production in *both* agriculture and industry will be required, it is nevertheless true that economic development will often lead to difficult problems of rural-urban balance. Famine can be avoided in the rapidly growing towns only if sufficient food is made available to meet the needs of their increasing populations. This food can come either from the rural areas of the country concerned or from abroad. The latter course will normally be unsuitable, for it will force a reduction in imports of investment goods, which are urgently needed to increase production in the poor countries.

The amount of food made available to the cities from the countryside basically depends, in a free-enterprise economy, on the individual decisions of farmers; they can eat the food they produce or they can sell it in order to secure money with which to save, to purchase goods, or to meet obligations such as taxation. In the past the farmer often preferred to eat his grain rather than sell it. The results of this preference have been particularly obvious in years of bad harvests. Throughout history there has been a tendency for the towns to be insufficiently supplied with food and for periodic shortages to occur.

Governments must ensure that the industrialized towns get enough food. The farmer must be encouraged to sell his crops rather than keep them to feed his family. He will do this voluntarily if he wishes either to save money or to buy consumption goods; he will be forced to do it if he has to pay taxes. What are the economic and social results of these three ways in which food can be brought to the towns, and which of these three methods can be used most successfully by governments? If the farmer wishes to save, he sells his crops and then lends the money to the state, to an individual, or to a firm, allowing them to use it for purposes of investment. This choice is fairly infrequent, largely because savings in monetary form are often unacceptable in the poor countries. People who produce more crops than they need usually buy certain forms of visible wealth: gold, silver, land, cattle, etc. These provide evidence of status and in times of distress can be sold. The idea that money itself could be saved seldom recommends itself to citizens of these countries. Governments will probably find it difficult to stimulate a rapid increase in saving, particularly as economic growth in the poor countries will almost inevitably be associated with inflation and a decline in the value of money.

Governments could increase voluntary sales of crops by encouraging farmers to develop new tastes for manufactured goods, which they cannot make for themselves. In order to secure such goods they would be forced to sell more of their crops. If they are unwilling to lower their consumption of food, they might use more land or try to get a larger crop from the land already cultivated. Thus the introduction of new tastes *can* act as an incentive to production; it may encourage the farmer to produce more food in order to be able to buy goods he wants. Nevertheless, such a policy has grave dangers; it would increase the demand for manufactured goods and as the demand is already larger than the supply this would increase dissatisfaction. The advisability of stimulating tastes in the rural areas will depend on the position of each country. If it can be expected that a rise in the level of tastes will lead to a substantial increase in the amount of work carried out—as may be the case in a country with surplus land—such a step might be advantageous. If the amount of land is limited and there is little possibility of increasing production through further work, it is unlikely that such a policy would be satisfactory.

The government can attempt to force the agriculturalist to sell an increased amount of food by taxing him. Such a step, however, may not be sucessful in raising the amount of food available in the towns, for the farmer may succeed in evading the tax or, if the burden is found too heavy, may decrease production rather than increase it. This occurred in Russia between the two World Wars, and a similar reaction has resulted in Eastern Europe on several occasions since the war. Attempts to tax farmers have often been opposed because of their low incomes. However, income figures are calculated in such a way as to overstate the difference in standards of living between rural and urban areas. In any case, the theoretical justice of taxation will not always be the determining factor; the need for food may sometimes force decisions.

The traditional preference of the economist for direct taxes — those based on the income of the individual — rather than indirect taxes, which increase the cost of goods and services purchased, has been carried over into discussions of the problems of the poor countries. This preference, however, is based on neoclassical economics, where it was claimed that the price of goods represented the cost of production and any interference with these prices would therefore decrease total production. As this is not true, for unemployment and a shortage of foreign exchange and capital distort the price structure in the poor countries, the preference for direct taxes is invalid. The advantages of indirect taxation, its relative unobtrusiveness and the fact that it has a smaller unfavorable effect on the amount of work carried out, come into their own. Some direct taxation will normally be needed to ensure that the richer members of society pay a larger share of the taxes, but indirect taxation will be preferable when money must be obtained from the poorer members of the country.

The problems of supplying food to an increasing urban population may be still further complicated by the desire and the need for land reform in many countries with the greatest population pressure. Peasant farmers and landless laborers very often want to obtain their own land. In many countries land reform acts have been passed restricting the acreage that may be owned by one person and distributing the land thus made available to the rural population. While such changes have normally added to its welfare, the general effect of the redistribution has been to reduce the amount of food sold to the towns. The richer farmer, cultivating a large area, will tend to send more food to market than the new owners will sell after the area has been divided into smaller farms; the wealthy man is more likely to buy manufactured goods, to be heavily taxed, and even to be willing to save. It may, however, be possible to avoid a decrease in the food supplied to the cities when there are large areas of unused land that can be distributed, but this situation is least likely to occur when the population is densest and the need for land reform usually greatest. Venezuela's land reform policies recognize these facts, and only uncultivated areas will be distributed.

The effects of land reform on total production of crops are disputed, partly because they vary from country to country and situation to situation. The farmer will normally be encouraged to work harder if he owns his own land, because a larger proportion of the benefits from his activity will accrue to him; conversely the reduction of farm size may decrease the efficiency of cultivation. The case for land reform and the exact manner in which it should be instituted cannot be discussed in general terms. Often the need for social reform is so urgent that the possible economic disadvantages will have to be accepted; although any reform should, of course, minimize the unfortunate effects.

It appears likely that one of the major difficulties that will continue to plague the governments in many of the poor countries for a long time will be the inability to obtain sufficient food for the urban population. Gifts of agricultural produce may therefore be one of the major ways in which the rich countries can help the poor. However, even if such aid were given, it will sometimes be necessary to reduce the flow of migrants from the country to the towns, a necessity pointed up by the fact that the arrival of people in the towns requires expenditure on housing and services. This money is often found by delaying or abandoning investment projects that could increase production.

Movement to the urban areas is due in part to their attraction, the belief that the "good life" can be lived only there, but it also results from the fact that existence in the rural areas in many parts of the world is becoming intolerable. Old values are being destroyed by the pressure of want, but no new social structure is being developed in their place. Unfortunately, the process of destruction is self-reinforcing; as conditions become worse and opportunities diminish, the more adventurous and the more intelligent leave. After their departure the possibility of evolving a satisfactory way of life in the rural areas is still further undermined because of the absence of the people who could help to renew it.

Attempts are being made to help the villager develop a new way of life by assisting him in the improvements he desires to make and by supplying the goods now felt to be essential for everyday living. Programs of this type have been introduced on a limited basis throughout the poor areas of the world, but they are hampered by the ubiquitous shortage of money. In many areas development schemes are also restricted because those who have lived in the cities are unwilling to work in the villages, while the members of the younger generation who have become convinced of the necessity and urgency of rural development are discouraged from doing this work by the attitudes of their parents, whose lives are governed by traditional ideas and ideals.

Conflict and dissatisfaction are also caused by the introduction of teachers trained in the towns into the more backward villages. If these teachers are given no special training they will inevitably inculcate in their pupils a desire for the comfortable, sophisticated urban life of their memories. In India, where the British developed an educational pattern appropriate to urban Britain, they created a group ill-fitted for present conditions in the Indian subcontinent. These are the discontented intellectuals, believing themselves unjustly deprived of the jobs to which their education should entitle them. There is a real danger that the adoption of Western educational patterns elsewhere can lead to a repetition of this wastage on a far wider scale. Many people who are brought up in the rural areas will have to live out their lives there. It is. therefore essential that the education they receive should provide employment for their energies and talents, and enable them to find fulfillment of their aspirations in the district where they were born.

Urban growth cannot continue at its present rate in the poor countries if social breakdown is to be prevented. Direct controls can be avoided only if the validity of rural life is preserved and employment opportunities provided. This may require that industry be developed in the rural areas rather than concentrated in the towns. The villages must participate in both the economic progress and sense of achievement of the rest of the country, if the most active and intelligent members of society are not to leave the rural areas.

If the poor countries are to formulate satisfactory policies, they must not be hypnotized by increases in the national income to the exclusion of all other factors. Coventional methods of calculation often introduce a favorable bias into estimates of increases in income, while ignoring many vitally important social factors. This view was clearly expressed at a conference by a delegate from one of the poor countries. It had been suggested that although conditions in the poor countries tended to result in inaccurate national income figures at the present time, the effect of economic growth would be to make the social patterns of the poor countries resemble those of the rich and the economic conventions would then become satisfactory. At this point the delegate broke in saying, "But we don't want to copy your civilization, we want to develop our own."

We have seen in this chapter that the process of development cannot be based simply on free competition, for this will lead to unnecessary unemployment and rural discontent. Governments will have to intervene in order to ensure that the best possible use is made of available resources. Their task will be greatly complicated by the shortage of trained civil servants and by the existence of problems far more complicated than those that occurred during the industrialization of the Western countries. The next chapter discusses the implication of political conditions and examines possible solutions.

V. *Will Western Forms of Democracy Be Workable?*

IN RECENT YEARS some newly independent nations that firmly proclaim their adherence to democratic beliefs have temporarily abandoned the institutions of democracy as they are understood in the West; others, who on assuming their independence adopted democratic beliefs, have publicly stated their doubts about the applicability of these principles to the problems they face; still others have refused from the beginning to accept Western democracy as appropriate to their existing problems. These developments have led to much discussion in the West; some suggest that, if the forms of Western democracy are not followed, countries will necessarily fail in their task; others argue that Western democracy cannot be expected to be suitable and that any attempt to apply it will necessarily lead to waste of resources and lack of governmental control.

There is sometimes a tendency to examine this problem

in moral terms. However, no form of government can be ideal; it must always be a compromise between liberty and control, an idea clearly expressed in the statement "Your liberty to swing your arm ends where my nose begins." The exact compromise between liberty and control must vary with the actual problems of the state; a greater degree of control and a lesser amount of liberty may well be acceptable and necessary in periods of external or internal stress than in periods of quiet. Western nations have been willing in the past to give greater powers to government in time of war than in time of peace; the problems the poor countries face at the present time suggest that a greater amount of control will have to be exercised than has been necessary in the rich countries in recent years.

The ideal of democracy is so often evoked it seems almost unnecessary to seek to define it, yet its outlines become hazy as one examines them. What are the distiguishing marks of democracy? Certainly not solely the ability to vote, but the knowledge that the possibility of voting can influence the policy and ideas of the government that is elected. If policies are set regardless of how votes are cast, universal suffer-age becomes a meaningless gesture. Neither do forms of government automatically ensure democracy. The English government, in theory, could easily be turned into a dicta-torship. The nucleus of government, the cabinet, determines policy and it is then voted upon by the House of Commons, but the majority party always follows the line laid down in the cabinet, for it is always the party in power that chooses the members of the cabinet from its own ranks. In the years since the war, even the gravest issues have failed to result in more than three or four members disobeying the party line, and their disobedience often resulted in expulsion from the party.

The system of government in America with its division

of powers could, in theory, result in a situation where no policy could be carried out—each group insisting that its own ideas should be accepted. Such a stalemate does not, in fact, occur. In France in the years following the war, the Fourth Republic was so "democratic" that efficient government proved impossible. There was a multiplicity of parties, each with a policy democratically determined by its members; however, in voting on an issue a member who disliked the decision made by his party was more or less free to vote as he pleased. Coalitions of parties were constantly made and unmade and the strain of endeavoring to hold together a diversified group of this type in order to have a consistent majority was so great that the average length of governments during the Fourth Republic was only five and a half months. Eventually the disadvantages of this pattern were considered so serious that the Fourth Republic was abolished and the Fifth set up with far greater powers concentrated in the President and the responsibilities of the Constituent Assembly and the Senate greatly curtailed; there was less "democracy" but better government.

However, even under the Fourth Republic the government of France was assured. There can be much debate about its efficiency but France's rate of economic growth was higher than ever before in her history. Despite theoretical possibilities the British Government remains a democracy and the American Government avoids a complete stalemate. However, in all these cases it is not only the expressed or written rules that prevent dangerous developments, but an unwritten and, in some cases, unformalized set of conventions that define the acceptable limits of action. These preserve the basic structure of government while allowing it to adapt to changing conditions. The mere transfer of *forms* of government cannot ensure that safeguards against misrule will be adopted at the same time. The unwritten conventions of politics, the things that are and are not permissible, vary from country to country, and unless the value-system is such that it supports rather than challenges the new form of government, it is likely to be ineffective. The aim of the poor countries must be to find ways of developing the correct policies. Western systems of government may not be most suitable for the task.

This problem and this aim were well expressed by Tom Mboya, chairman of the All-African People's Conference, in an article written after touring the United States in an effort to correct ideas about the contemporary African scene. "Some non-Africans are concerned about the development of opposition parties and others about the forms that governmental institutions will take. Many people seem to expect that Africa must keep what she inherits from her former colonial masters. Africa cannot, however, for very obvious reasons, adopt a blueprint of European or American institutions. Her governmental institutions must recognize Africa's cultural and social background and must move away from the forms used by the colonial powers—fitted for indirect rule—to a representative system."

The type of government adopted must be designed to deal with the particular problems the poor countries face. Three issues will dominate in coming years. First, the attempt to secure economic growth; this is essential if the increase in population is not to lead to a decline in the standard of living and if "the revolution of rising expectations" is to be satisfied. Second, the need to change the attitudes of these countries to bring them into accord with modern conditions; while work and saving must not be worshiped as they have sometimes been in the West, more attention must be given to them. The attempt to meet these two aims will be complicated in many areas by a third requirement, the need to destroy existing social organizations, such as the caste system in India and tribal enmity in Africa, and to weld separate and often traditionally hostile groups into a nation.

These problems are far more complex than those faced by the rich countries in their early stages of economic growth. Adam Smith's influence was at its height and it was believed that he had shown that the self-interested decisions of each individual would lead to the maximum posible rate of growth in the economy and in the welfare of society. Governments did not interfere with the supply of foreign exchange and the level of employment. The "economic system" was presumed to deal with these maters, and if there *was* unemployment and suffering it was thought that any government action could only worsen the situation, for it would interfere with the "immutable" laws of economics.

Governments now recognize that their actions can affect the amount of production, employment, imports and exports. The poor countries are therefore faced with tasks the rich countries did not recognize in the early stages of growth because of the differences in social theory and the relative lack of a social conscience during the nineteenth century. It is, of course, true that the rich countries also have to design economic policies at present, but this is a less crucial problem for them; there are more trained and educated personnel available, and the results of waste and inefficiency are less damaging. Even if some time, money, and talent were wasted by the process of nationalizing and denationalizing the steel industry, as was the case in England, this is less serious that the effect of a comparable amount of waste in one of the poor countries. For in an economy in the first stages of growth there is little margin that can be used for investment.

In most poor countries *all* the possible policies will be unpleasant. For example, critics will be able to claim either

that too much money and effort are being spent on investment, and that the starving inhabitants are therefore being
deprived of the food they require in order to live; or, alternatively, that the country is investing too little and conse-
quently insufficient provision is being made for the economic
growth essential if the necessary resources to take care of
the rising population are to be available in the future. In
commenting upon decisions it will be essential to remember
that economic growth cannot be obtained without sacrifice;
the amount of sacrifice essential in any particular case will
be difficult to determine. The *only* cetainty is that the poor
countries will be forced to adopt new, and often unpleasant
policies if they are to deal with the issues they face.

The most difficult problem for the governments of many
countries is to find the right relationship between economic
growth and the past and future values of the society. Change
will be required in order to secure economic growth, but in
which direction and how fast should it proceed? There is
no way to "prove" the right set of values in any society; it
depends on past history and present aims as well as the future toward which the country aspires. All we can know is
that a mere parroting of the values of the rich countries will
not be suitable; there is doubt in the rich countries themselves about many of the after-effects of urbanization and
the specialization of labor. Effort is now being devoted to
finding ways of overcoming their unfavorable effects. The
values of the West are continually changing: the adoption
of present attitudes that are not even appropriate to today's
technology and social attitudes — let alone tomorrow's —
would seriously hamper the poor countries.

These nations can only decide on the appropriate actions
after they have developed their policy goals. They cannot
progress without a plan — however loose it may be — but
their difficulty in devising it cannot be overestimated. Much

Western comment has been impatient of ideological discussion, claiming it to be a waste of time. It is forgotten that the values and sense of purpose of the Western countries were developed over decades and centuries and that the range of actions open to these countries is therefore limited by their past history—an unwritten plan already exists. The poor countries, as they try to hurtle themselves into the twentieth century, seem to their leaders to be confronted by a wide range of possibilities. A sense of national purpose must be developed, but there are few guidelines for the search.

Dictatorial power can build this sense of national purpose; policies are then imposed by a single ruler or a ruling clique. Such a solution has always been condemned in the West, but it is the *goal* of good government that is important not solely the form of the institutions by which it is attained. There is some evidence that the governments of the countries that have changed in recent years from Western democracy to a form of dictatorship have become less corrupt and more efficient, while the rights of the inhabitants of the country often appear to be more secure. The West has always argued that dictatorship, however efficient it may be in the short run, must inevitably fail. Its view is clearly expressed in one of the most famous political aphorisms of all time: "Power corrupts, absolute power corrupts absolutely." This belief, however, is based on the existence of Western values and is not necessarily appropriate in other areas where power is not sought but only accepted. Despite the problems they raise, it would appear that dictatorships, either overt or covert, will remain a common form of government in the poor countries for many years.

Another method that the poor countries have sometimes used to deal with their particular problems has caused much misunderstanding in the past. These nations deny the wis-

dom of Western political systems and do not accept that
each person should consult his own interests or those of the
people or institutions he represents when determining policy;
voting in favor of a measure if it would be favorable to him
or his constituents, and against if it would be unsatisfactory
from these points of view. They claim that this method of
making decisions results in partial judgment and unnecessary
tensions between conflicting groups. They argue that government policies should be based on unanimous decisions, and
that if unanimity can be attained the course of action decided
upon will be more satisfactory for all concerned.

This belief is not confined to the poor countries. Such
methods were used by the Joint Chiefs of Staff during the
war and are the basis for Quaker philosophy. Certain firms
require their committees to make decisions by unanimous
vote. What is the necessary condition for such unanimity?
Each of the members of the group must consider its goal to
be more important than anything else, including his own
selfish advantage, and be willing to give up personal and
sectional interests that conflict with the main goal. The
Joint Chiefs of Staff found that the need to win the war
overcame the problems of service rivalry that in peacetime
occasionally make complete agreement impossible. In a
firm, the desire to ensure that it improves its position as
rapidly as possible can provide a goal to unite the committee
members. The necessary condition for agreement can be
made clearer by an example. It would be useless for a pro-
hibition committee to hope for agreement if one of its
members considered that drink was no evil; on the other
hand, a committee for the suppression of drunkenness might
succeed in producing a unanimous report even though one
of its members was a brewer; he might believe that the
suppression of drunkenness was more important than his

profits, or that drunkenness would affect unfavorably the future profits of his business.

There appears to be no obvious reason why the welfare of a country could not be placed above that of sectional interests—a country might therefore be controlled by unanimous decisions. Unanimity would be reached, not as a result of dictation by one member of the group, but because of the group's determination to seek out the best policy for the country. This method proved feasible in some North American tribes where decisions were made by all the elders of the tribe; if unanimity could not be attained, this was not assumed to indicate that one or more members of the group should be overruled but that there was a genuine difference of opinion. No action was taken until this difference could be resolved. There have even been occasions where international bodies have required a unanimous vote before action could be taken and where this requirement has not paralyzed the organization. This was particularly true of the Organization for European Economic Cooperation which was a vital force in the recovery of Europe from World War II.

It will, of course, be difficult to ensure satisfactory functioning in such a group, but often no more impossible than to secure the proper working of Western democracy. This concept of government will have its advantages, for it does not claim that the pursuit of man's selfish interests will necessarily result in the good of the community. Among the non-communist powers, Indonesia in particular is striving to use this approach, basing it upon the methods of control previously used in the village communities. Several African states are also considering its applicability to their problems.

The West has been unwilling to accept that such a form of government can be democratic because of the absence of an opposition party. However, an opposition party—

which must, by definition, oppose—may often be inappropriate in the poor countries. As Tom Mboya argues in the
article quoted earlier: "To suggest that the popular leaders
who combine during the struggle for liberation should break
up and form different parties because the book so requires
is not only reckless but to ignore the urgent problems that
a new state faces. The solution to these problems requires a
stable government that can also offer security for expanded
economic growth. The responsibility thrust on the shoulders
of both the party in power and the often weak, ineffective
opposition party is tremendous and one which requires
strength of character, honesty of purpose and, above all, a
deep conviction in the service of the country and the
people."*

The amount of power delegated to the central government
will need to be far greater than in the early stages of industrial growth in the countries that are now rich. It is, however, possible that the governments of the poor countries
can limit their responsibilities by allowing considerable
autonomy in the rural areas. Community development programs, for example, have usually attained the best results
when people have been allowed to choose the projects that
seemed vital to them, rather than when forced to carry out
proposals made by the central government; the latter, town-
oriented, may be unable to appreciate the real needs of the
rural areas. We saw, for example, that suggestions for the
introduction of piped water and higher-yielding wheat
failed to be accepted because they did not meet the felt
needs of the population.

The policies developed by the central government must
be presented so that they will be seen to be acceptable. As
they will often conflict with traditional beliefs, a method must
be found of "educating" the population to accept them. Such
a suggestion raises specters the West has sought to exorcise

—it raises the prospect that governments will "propagandize" their populations to accept new ideas. However, the need for changed values is so urgent that only deliberate planned action can bring it about rapidly enough. The presently accepted goals of the poor countries are no longer adequate to provide for the survival of the community or of the people within it; new values are necessary and these must be taught.

The introduction of a new set of values into the poor countries will largely be done by the schools or at least by people from outside the area, for parents will instill the beliefs traditionally held in the community. Any deliberate attempt to introduce new ideas will inevitably strain the relations between parents and children; the older members of society find it difficult and often illogical to change their ideas about the right way of life. One of the challenges that will face the educator is to find methods that will allow the younger generation to learn and appreciate new values but not cause so wide a gulf between the older and younger generations that society breaks down completely. This task will be further complicated by the need to destroy old hostilities between conflicting groups and avoid the emergence of new ones.

How can the educational curriculum be decided? We saw that it was essential for the rural way of life to be validated rather than ridiculed when compared with the urban areas. But who can decide exactly what should be taught? It is certain that unanimity cannot be reached easily, for the values imparted will be one of the major factors in determining the speed and direction of progress. However, the result of too much discussion will be to make it impossible for teachers to discern the goals toward which the country is aiming. Frequent changes in ideas can only result in a sense of flux and frustration in those who are attempting to implement the resulting policies. Decisions will often have to be made by the central authorities and in certain countries it may be necessary to impose some limitations to criticism.

In time of war, the right to discuss government policies is curtailed and this restraint on individual liberty is generally accepted by the public. It is not an exaggeration to say that the poor countries are fighting for their very existence, that the problems faced by their governments are so great that the odds against success are already heavy. They, therefore, need the same rights as are granted to governments in time of war, in order to control dissension for the sake of personal aggrandizement. Such a conclusion is undoubtedly fundamentally unpleasant to many in the West. It is, however, certainly better to accept this fact and be able to understand the reasons behind the policies of the poor countries than to criticize them for taking actions that are unavoidable.

There will be no easy way of judging whether the steps taken in the poor countries are those that are most appropriate; our estimate must rest on an examination of the economic, social, and political possibilities. This has implications in terms of international relations. At present the United States and certain other countries refuse to recognize a nation if they feel that its policies are not in the best interests of its people or of the world community of nations. If this policy is to be logical, the United States must believe that her judgment of the situation and the possibilities open to the other government are more reliable than that of the leaders of the country concerned. Such an attitude will seldom be justified. The only satisfactory method of determining whether a country is entitled to international recognition will be to examine whether it has firm control over its territory; this method is already followed by a large number of states. Such a policy has its own advantages, for it separates the ideological support of a country from the process of recognition. In addition, it allows nations that disapprove of the internal policies of another country to bring diplomatic pressure to bear and suggest that other more appropriate steps could be devised to meet its goals.

The stereotypes of the West about the "right" form of government are no longer adequate; each situation in the poor countries will need to be evaluated on its merits. There can be little doubt that the rulers of the great majority of the poor countries are now concerned to give their populations the maximum of freedom, combined with the most rapid, feasible rate of economic growth—despite this they will often be forced to take steps that curtail the amount of civil liberties. The rich countries must understand that these steps are the results of pressures unknown to them and that the policies followed are normally the *least unpleasant* available to the rulers of the poor countries—not those they would ideally adopt if conditions permitted.

VI. *Steps toward Economic Growth*

T HE PREVIOUS CHAPTERS have examined the political and social problems and policies in the poor countries. This chapter is concerned with the more strictly "economic" actions they can take at the present time. We begin the chapter with an examination of the rate of economic growth that could be achieved, and then discuss the effect of rising tastes and an increasing population on the need for growth. The different possible methods of increasing the rate of growth are then examined and the best hope for more rapid development is shown to depend on the use of unemployed labor.

Since the Second World War economic growth in the poor countries has in many cases only just kept up with, and in some cases even fallen behind, the rate of increase in population; as a result the gap between the incomes of the rich and poor countries has grown wider. What are the prospects for the future? Some indication may be obtained by examining the experience of countries during the course of development. Calculation of rates of growth depends, as we have already seen, on the conventions adopted, but it may be suggested that the rate of growth in America and much of Europe during the second half of the nineteenth century and the early twentieth was about 2 per cent per year. The American economy continued to grow between the two World Wars while there was almost general stagnation in Europe. The rate of growth in all countries has been more rapid since the Second World War and has normally been somewhere between 3 and 6 per cent per year in all the rich countries. In Russia growth in recent years has been at a rate of about 6 per cent per year and similar results have been achieved and sometimes surpassed in a few poor countries—although these results should be treated with caution, for the conventions adopted exaggerate progress in the early stages of development. It seems probable that the most rapid rise in production in recent years has been in China, following its intensive use of previously unemployed labor, but the information available is not sufficient to make it possible to calculate an exact rate of growth.

It can be estimated as a rough rule of thumb that in order to achieve a 1-per-cent increase in national income 2 to 4 per cent of the national income must be spent on investment—the production of tools, equipment, etc., that will make it possible to produce more goods at a later date. Thus a rate of growth of 3 per cent per year requires the expenditure of 6-12 per cent of the national income on investment, a rate of 7 per cent requires the investment of from 14-28 per cent of the national income, and a 10 per-cent increase per year would require the investment of from 20-40 per cent of the national income. If population is increasing, not all the benefits from the growth will accrue to the existing population, for the total income will have to be distributed among a larger number of people. If investment is to be carried out, the population of the country must be either willing or coerced to forego present goods in order to obtain additional goods in future years. They may voluntarily lend their money, they may be forced to pay taxes to support investment, they may do either voluntary or compulsory unpaid labor; in addition, firms may use part of their profits for investment rather than distribute this money to their owners.

The fastest conceivable rate of increase in income per head obtainable in most poor countries in the future might be around 5 per cent per year. A 5-per-cent rate of growth will require the investment of between 10 and 20 per cent of the national income—even if no population growth is taking place—and between 15 and 30 per cent assuming a 2-per-cent increase per year in population. These figures are greatly in excess of investment in most of the poor countries up to now—rates are often as low as 10 or even 5 per cent. Even in the rich countries the amount of investment seldom rises above 25 per cent. A more rapid rate of increase may be possible in some mineral-rich countries, and in those areas with climates particularly suited to certain crops. In most cases, however, the attainment of a higher rate of growth—and, indeed, of a 5-per-cent rate—will depend on an increase in the amount of aid given by the rich countries to the poor.

A rate of increase of 5 per cent per year in income per head would result in incomes about two and a half times as large in 1980 as they are today, and about seven times as large in the year 2000. However, the absolute gap between the incomes of the rich and poor countries would continue to widen during much, if not all, of this period. It is not suggested that these figures are exact; their object is to show that even on the most optimistic assumptions the problems of the poor countries cannot be solved in the next few years, whatever steps may be taken, and that the gap between income per head in the rich and poor countries must be expected to widen for several decades. If the assumption of a 5-per-cent growth rate is abandoned and present trends are examined, it would appear that the rate of growth in many countries will continue to be insufficient even to offset the rise in population unless greatly increased help is given from abroad.

Economic growth has become essential in the poor countries because of two major changes. One is the rapidly increasing desire for more goods and better education. A popular Ghanese song provides evidence of the revolution —the ideal man to marry is now one with a "car-ful, fridge-ful, been-to," the man who owns a car and a refrigerator, and has been abroad. Population increase provides the second reason; the rapidly declining death rate and the often stable birth rate have produced a "population explosion." Two possibilities will be open to these countries to avoid the breakdown of their societies, that might otherwise occur because of an inadequate rate of growth: they can either increase its rate or they can try to decrease the need for it. As it would appear that the rate of economic growth will not rise fast enough to meet all desires, the possibility of reducing the need for growth must also be examined. In fact, the necessity to limit population increase is slowly being accepted, but the possibility of ensuring that the desire for a higher material standard of living does not increase more rapidly than it can be satisfied is still hardly discussed.

Little attention has been paid by social scientists to the process of accepting new wants; the very fact that a rise in the standard of living has normally been felt to be good in itself has limited interest in this subject. Such a view about the importance of a rising material standard of living is not universal—it has been argued that happiness is not a function of the standard of living but of the proportion of the person's desires that can be satisfied. If this is true, the family that has few goods and is satisfied can be considered better off than one that has a larger income but is unable to meet its desires.

New wants can develop only as people gain knowledge of the existence of other goods. The major ways in which this happens in the poor countries are through contact with members of the richer countries who possess goods—whose very existence was previously unknown—and through the medium of films and advertisements in magazines. Such contacts are to some extent inevitable, but in addition an attempt is sometimes made to "sell" the rich countries to the poor by exhibiting advanced products. The Japanese ambassador, confronted with a traveling show of this type at its preview in Washington, asked that it should not be sent to Japan unless the United States were willing to supply the goods exhibited to all the Japanese who attended the show. He argued that it would be many years before the average Japanese would be able to reach such a standard of living and the exhibition could only promote discontent.

Local advertising aided by high-powered salesmanship is the other main force that acts to develop new tastes. Time-payment plans have also been introduced despite the fact that they can only be harmful in countries that suffer from an acute shortage of goods, for they allow people to purchase consumer goods before income has been earned. It is necessary for governments to consider how advertising and time-payment plans should be controlled in the poor countries. This control may not act to limit well-being, as would generally be expected in the West, it may actually increase it.

The acquiring of new wants has in many cases resulted in the abandonment of purchases more necessary to well-being. Primitive tribes are often considered ill-fed, but a survey showed that the health of these tribes was often better than that of societies that had met the impact of a money economy to a greater extent. An examination of 209 tribes selected as "primitive" showed that only twelve had diets deficient in both energy and protective foods, seven had diets deficient in energy foods only, and the remaining 190 had diets adequate for the lives they were leading. On the other hand, most of Asia and about half of Africa and South America had diets deficient in both energy and protective foods.

The fact that the introduction of new and attractive goods leads people to neglect more essential purchases should not be found surprising. The less practice families have had in choosing between one type of goods and another, the less sensible they will be in making purchases. While a person within a rich country may be able to compare the value of goods, deciding which he will purchase now, which later, and which he would buy if he received a raise in salary, this will not be true in many parts of the poor countries. People in the rich countries are used to choices and are able to make them rationally; they are used to advertising and may sometimes profit by it. It took time to develop these attitudes; it is foolish to expect the poor countries to possess them instinctively.

The other method of decreasing the need for economic growth is to limit the rate of population increase. Any suggestion that the rate of population growth should be lessened is violently opposed by certain groups. Some deny that such a program could work, stating that people would be unwilling to reduce the size of their families. Such arguments ignore the dramatic success of a program in Japan, where the birth rate has been halved within a decade, as well as studies made on these subjects in certain other areas of the world. These show that, given the opportunity, parents in most parts of the world would be willing to limit the size of their families. Included in their number are many who, because of religious views or traditional values, might have been expected to oppose such a step.

The essential opposition to contraception, however, is not based on logical argument but on a belief that it prevents the birth of an individual with a soul. It would be impossible to discuss this view here; one can only mention certain facts that must be taken into account. The practice of death control is now widespread, and where death rates have fallen the level of birth rates to be expected without contraception would result in a growth of population at a rate of about 3 per cent per year or more—a 3 per-cent rate would result in the doubling of the population every twenty-four years. Many of the poor countries cannot provide sufficient food, clothing, and shelter for such an increase; at some stage, therefore, death rates would be forced up again as a result of famine, unless the population was succored by outside help. But even if this help should be available to avoid a catastrophe, the population of the world could not double every twenty-four years for an extended period. Already in many areas of the world every scrap of land is cultivated and there is no privacy. Mankind has changed too many of the "natural" conditions on earth to refuse now to take action that would limit the rate of increase in population.

Some people who are willing to accept the argument set out in the last paragraph nevertheless believe that money spent on birth control is wasted, as all efforts to introduce it in the poor countries have been unsatisfactory; at the present time this is more or less true. This does not mean, however, that birth control is impracticable, but rather that there is a need for a low-cost oral contraceptive. Some progress has been reported in this direction, but the amount of money available for such work has been very small, certainly insufficient for rapid development and mass production. Even when a suitable chemical formula has been determined, many years must pass before it can be used on a large scale because of the possibility of dangerous side effects.

It is easy to understand the forces preventing a crash program in this field. There are many who disapprove of any action and others who are unaware of the urgency of the problem. Many who would be willing to expedite programs hesitate to do so for fear of distressing others. Nevertheless, there is some evidence of a change in attitudes. The Draper Committee, set up by the President of the United States to advise on the changes required in foreign-aid programs, proposed in 1959 that the United States should assist countries that ask for aid to deal with "the problem of rapid population growth."

The favorable effect on economic growth of limiting the rate of increase in population and in tastes should not be exaggerated, although it may well be that the degree of success in these fields will determine whether the poor countries are able to avoid complete breakdown in their social structure; without limitations the best efforts of governments may be overwhelmed. However, the impact of birth control can assume importance only a decade or more after a program has been adopted, while action to limit the rise in tastes can only hope to stop the "revolution of rising expectations" from getting completely out of hand.

We must, therefore, consider what economic steps can be taken by the government to increase the rate of growth. Many suggestions currently put forward rest on a misunderstanding of the essential problems facing these countries— it is often assumed that solutions to problems in the poor and rich countries must be identical. It is, however, insufficient to "assume" either that the same problems will be present or, if they are, that the solution of the rich country will be appropriate in the poor. For example, governments in the poor countries are often criticized for taking action in fields that are usually controlled by private enterprise in the rich countries. This censure is unreasonable because one of the most important reasons for the slow pace of economic growth in the poor countries is the shortage of entrepreneurs. The government must therefore act because private firms are unwilling to take the necessary steps.

The small number of educated people in most poor countries will be inadequate for all the pressing tasks; the government should not pre-empt more industrial activity than is absolutely necessary; those willing to work in private enterprise should be allowed to do so. The government will also be wise to limit its intervention in the market as much as possible, for a fully planned economy requires an extremely large administration and considerable expertise, but failure in planning will cause overproduction of some products and consequent waste; insufficient production of others. The most satisfactory way of restricting demand will be by price, but prices will have to be adjusted by the use of indirect taxes. It is not suggested that rationing by price is necessarily the fairest means of distribution but allocation by any other method requires greater control than is normally practicable, for it results in shortages of goods, from which some people will always try to profit. One experience in Indonesia will illustrate the point. A limited quantity of cloth was imported to meet an acute shortage and each person was allowed to purchase a small amount at a price below that which would have limited the demand to the amount available. Merchants hired people to stand in line, giving them enough money to buy the cloth and a small sum for the amount of time they stood there. When supplies were exhausted, the merchants resold the cloth at inflated prices. The profits from the scarcity accrued to one group in the community.

In previous chapters we have discussed some of the factors that determine the rate of growth. The most crucial is the attitude of the population toward work and leisure, consumption and saving; these can alter, but the rate of change will normally be relatively slow. Entrepreneurs can increase efficiency in their firms and factories—enabling more goods to be produced with the same amount of work, but in most of the poor countries few entrepreneurs are interested in getting maximum efficiency in their factories; the amount of effort they are willing to put into reorganizing them is limited. Investment can be increased as people save more money and firms distribute a smaller proportion of their profits to stockholders, using more to build new factories and buy equipment, but these sums are unlikely to be large enough to produce a satisfactory rate of growth.

There are two further possibilities we have not yet discussed. People can produce investment goods in time that would otherwise be unused; the many unemployed and underemployed people in these countries could be put to work. Second, available scientific knowledge might be used to increase production. This possibility, however, depends on new information being made available in forms suitable for use in the poor countries. The results of increases in technical knowledge are normally incorporated in complicated and expensive machines, their use profitable in the rich areas with relative abundance of capital and shortage of labor. They will normally be unsuited for areas where there is unemployed labor and a shortage of capital, as well as few mechanical skills. Special steps must be taken to design inexpensive tools and instruments suitable for use by the large labor forces in the poor countries before they will be able to take full advantage of the scientific knowledge available. The use of technological information is also hampered by the frequent insistence of many poor countries on large-scale investments for reasons of prestige, rather than scattering smaller enterprises throughout the country that would limit transportation and other problems.

The greatest potential for increased production in these countries is the use of time not already employed in productive activity; people can join together in building schools, dams, roads, etc. Community development programs have therefore been set up in many parts of the world. Villages are encouraged to undertake voluntary work to improve conditions and increase their opportunities. Governments provide personnel and sometimes a small amount of materials or money, but most of the funds are normally obtained from the community itself and work is unpaid. Such programs have contributed to the building of houses, dispensaries, and schools, the construction and paving of roads, the digging of wells, and many other desirable goals.

However, the amount of work people are prepared to contribute on a voluntary basis is limited, particularly in those areas where the concept of money wages has developed. A major contribution to growth can be obtained only if those who are presently unemployed or underemployed are brought into the labor force. This will normally require that wages are paid for the work done. What will be the results of this step? If people can be put to work to produce goods that other people wish to buy, such as cotton cloth, this will cause a rise in the standard of living. The increase in the amount of wages paid out, and therefore in the amount of goods people are able to purchase, will be balanced by an increased quantity of goods that can be bought. However, the major problem in many of these countries is that the labor force cannot find work because there are too few factory jobs and no land for cultivation; the need is to increase investment and thus increase the number of available jobs. However, when people are employed to produce dams or build factories, the payment of wages is not offset immediately by a rise in the amount of goods available for purchase; this occurs only after the investment has been completed and productive capacity augmented.

To illustrate, let us assume that a dam is to be built and that payments to the labor force will constitute by far the largest part of the total cost. The construction of the dam will be a net gain to the economy, for instead of people being idle they will be employed on a project that will eventually increase the amount of crops. But inflationary pressure will normally result unless the current payments to the newly employed workers can be offset by a decrease in the amount of money spent by others.

Up to the time that the unemployed workers are hired to work on the dam their minimum food and clothing needs were met by their friends or relatives, for very few governments in the poor countries support the unemployed. When they obtain jobs, they will be paid wages by their employer, but this does not mean that extra food and clothing will be made available in response to the extra demand that will result as they try to spend their earnings. The families who previously supported them will not normally cut their purchases, for their incomes will not have been reduced; they will share the same amount of goods among a smaller number of people. Little additional food or goods will therefore be available on the market to satisfy the demand of those newly employed in producing investment goods. There will be a larger demand for existing supplies, merchants will be able to set higher prices on their goods; this increase in prices will lead to demands for higher wages and further increases in price.

Inflation of this classical pattern will not take place if the amount of goods people wish, and are able to purchase, is approximately equal to the amount available for sale. If, therefore, the government or a firm employs men who were previously idle to produce investment goods such as dams, some method of cutting down demand elsewhere in the economy must be found if inflation is to be avoided. Any increase in savings would help to achieve this result, but voluntary savings will normally be insufficient in the poor countries. Is there any way in which the government can avoid inflation and still secure the necessary economic growth? In the next few pages we will explore the methods economists have suggested to limit the demand for goods to the level of supply, and will suggest that new ideas will be needed if the amount of inflation in the poor countries is to be reduced to a minimum.

The classical suggestions made by economists to limit inflation are increased taxes and credit control. It is ironical that higher taxation is proposed as a means of obtaining more rapid economic growth in the poor countries, for in the past one of the basic economic theories was that an increase in taxation would decrease the amount of effort people made and therefore reduce the rate of growth. Economists argued that the result of an increase in taxation would be a decrease in the amount of work carried out— that, as people balance the unpleasantness of labor against the amount of money they obtain from doing it, the result of a lowered after-tax wage would certainly be a smaller amount of work. This reaction did not follow the increase in tax rates in the rich countries during the war; a study made by the Harvard Business School showed that men normally took little notice of the level of taxation when deciding on the amount of work they did. Economic theory appeared to contradict the known facts; it was therefore suggested that the theory was wrong and heavy taxation should not be expected to lead to a decrease in the amount of work.

This revised theory was then carried over to the poor countries, and since they were in need of more money for investment it was argued that the best way to obtain it was to raise taxes. Western economists encouraged the poor countries to impose high rates, which sometimes meant that people would be worse off if they worked than if they did nothing. However, the reaction to increases in taxes is different in the rich and poor countries. In the rich countries the larger part of the professional and managerial classes like work or desire the prestige it brings—they balance the satisfaction gained from labor against the satisfaction from other forms of activity. Thus, a change in income does not have a major effect on the amount of work done. Work is also encouraged by the urgent desire to obtain a higher standard of living. In the poor countries, where most people balance the dissatisfaction of working against the satisfaction of consumption and saving, an increase in the level of taxation will often reduce the amount of effort made to reach a higher standard of living.

High taxes in poor countries, therefore, discourage work and thus decrease the rate of growth in the economy. This, however, is not the only unfavorable result. If people are taxed at high rates, they will cease to save as much as before, for they will often attach more importance to safeguarding their standard of living than to preserving their level of saving. Some people may even choose to use part of the resources they have already saved to prevent a decline in their standard of living. There would, therefore, be a decrease in the amount of money made available for private investment, which will offset the sum obtained by the government through increased taxation. In addition, the imposition of tax rates that are generally considered unreasonably high will encourage a search for loopholes in the tax laws and dishonesty in compiling tax returns. It therefore seems that while progressive taxation is necessary in the poor countries, the imposition of too heavy burdens will decrease rather than increase the possible rate of growth. The use of high taxes to avoid inflation will normally be ineffective; such success as is achieved will be at the cost of limiting or abolishing economic growth.

One further point about forms of taxation should be made here. The effect of direct taxation—income taxes—is to reduce the amount of resources a man has available but leaves him free to spend his money as he wishes. A rich man may decide to reduce the number of servants he employs and continue to buy the same amount of scarce imported goods. The benefit of this step to the economy will be limited, for his servants will join the ranks of the unemployed or underemployed. On the other hand, the demand for goods in short supply—especially those imported from abroad—will not be decreased. In the poor countries the tax structure should be used to increase the cost of items in short supply. In particular, the price of luxury goods imported from abroad should reflect the shortage of foreign exchange.

The second suggestion made by economists, that credit control can be used to limit inflation in the poor countries, can be more rapidly dismissed. The need in the poor countries is to increase investment in order to achieve economic growth; the object of credit control is to limit the amount of money available and therefore cut expenditures. It would be possible for credit control to play a major role in limiting inflation while allowing economic growth to continue, if demands for credit for consumption and for investment purposes could be distinguished, applications for investment purposes being treated favorably and those for consumption purposes refused. Even the rich countries have not been able to devise satisfactory mechanisms to reach this goal; it is therefore unlikely that any way can be found in the poor countries where banking institutions are far less well organized.

The economic remedies proposed for inflation in the poor countries have very limited application; they cannot control it without diminishing or preventing growth. If inflationary pressure is compounded by labor unions' attempts to push up wages at a faster rate than the increase in productivity, these traditional remedies will be even less effective. The proposals for counterinflationary policy in the poor countries are based on neoclassical economics, which does not consider the problems of growth. However, in the real world where the attainment of economic development is the most vital problem, the unfavorable effects of these economic actions will normally be greater than the advantages they bring. It will not normally be possible to obtain the needed rate of economic growth without some inflation.

Are there any other ways in which growth can be encouraged and inflation lessened? One method has been employed extensively and its use is growing: the practice of encouraging people to volunteer their labor for certain investment projects in a village or rural area. Another possibility is to return to methods of an earlier day and impose a labor tax. Instead of the whole tax obligation being determined in money terms, part could be expressed in a duty to work a certain number of days a year—with a possibility of discharging this liability by payment of a sum of money equivalent to the daily income of the worker multiplied by the number of workdays. Those already employed would probably normally prefer to pay the tax rather than be absent from their jobs, while the unemployed would prefer to do the work. The receipts from those who preferred to pay in money would make it possible to use some of the previously unemployed on investment projects without creating any inflationary pressure.

It seems to be generally agreed in the West that "forced labor" is wrong. Yet once the necessity of taxation has been accepted it seems possible that this proposal will be more just than the head tax, which is still levied, or even income taxes. For money taxes require that each person be able to earn money, and the resulting competition for jobs increases the power of employers, who, as a result, can pay low wages. Each person subject to the head tax *must* earn a certain amount of money each year. On the other hand, a labor tax would allow the individual to satisfy his obligation to the state with a certain number of days of work near his home, while if the work seemed unpleasing to him he could pay the tax in money instead. Historically, perhaps the most important reason for the banning of forced labor was the brutality of those who supervised it; it is probable that at present the governments of the poor countries would be less demanding than the private employers of many workers. The bias in the West against forced labor results from a comfortable belief that money taxation does not infringe the rights of the citizen, while a labor tax would. In fact, the income tax is basically a labor tax, but it is more convenient for the state to collect it in money form; in the poor countries a straight labor tax may very often be more suitable.

It might be argued that the work done under such a program would not be done enthusiastically, that the worker would look upon it as an unwarranted interference with his freedom of action. Such an idea is partly due to Western patterns of thought. It seems probable that, in some of the countries where independence has recently been achieved, compulsory labor might provide a method of drawing the country together rather than splitting it apart; these countries might even demand that all the inhabitants participate rather than allowing commutation of the tax on a money basis. This suggestion is made to dramatize the fact that economic policies thought hopelessly out of date may still be suitable in the poor countries. The undoubted success of China in her program of industrialization and in increasing agricultural productivity has been based primarily on her use of previously unemployed labor. Available information about the methods employed and the result achieved is not sufficient to make a reliable evaluation of how much has been accomplished or of the reactions of the workers themselves. It would, however, be unrealistic not to recognize that the lengthening of the work week and the use of all available labor resources have made possible a great increase in both industrial and agricultural production. This has led several other poor countries to consider the relevance of this step.

To those countries with large exports of a single commodity, one further possibility is open. The government can constitute itself sole exporter of the product, buying it at a relatively low fixed price and selling it at the higher world price. The difference between receipts and expenditure can be used for investment purposes. This policy has been successfully applied in Ghana, where the amount received by the cocoa farmer has typically been less than half of the world price. Although this policy has been condemned by some, either on the grounds that it interferes with free competition or that it is too heavy a penalty for the cocoa producer, it is probable that this is the most effective and least unjust method of raising money in these countries where it is applicable. It must be judged not in the context of "right" or "wrong," but as being the least unpleasant available alternative.

Whatever the steps taken by most of the poor countries, it is unlikely that inflation can be completely avoided if economic growth is to be achieved. Stable prices could be maintained only if sufficient money were transferred from purchases of consumption goods to pay for investment or if additional unpaid work were carried out. These steps will usually not take place voluntarily, and the measures that can be adopted by governments will be limited unless the economy is completely planned. We will find in Part III, however, that the transfer of resources through foreign aid can help these countries to achieve growth with relatively stable prices.

Before we leave the subject of the poor countries a brief summary may be useful. We have discussed the need of the poor countries for economic growth and the often-overwhelming difficulty of achieving it. We have seen that economic growth is not the only goal for these countries, and that change to bring about economic improvements must be engineered in such a way that the established living patterns of the people are not completely destroyed.

The rate of economic development can be approximately measured by the increase in national income, although the economists' conventions often overstate the gain that occurs during the process of industrialization. The decline in happiness that may result from this process is incalculable. Those who claim successes in the economic field are therefore able to support their contentions with figures, while those who hope to preserve traditional values have to rely on argument by illustration alone. As figures often speak louder than words in the modern world, those who try to preserve the fabric of society will be at a disadvantage. In addition, they will be fighting against what the proponents of economic growth will always label as "progress" and be in the unenviable position of defending what already exists.

Finally, while the causal relationship between industrialization and a higher national income is generally understood and accepted, its relation to the disintegration of a society and to mental ill-health is a more recent discovery, and its implications have been relatively little explored. Nevertheless, an appreciation of the intimate causal connection is growing. Dr. Branko Kesic, professor of hygiene and social medicine at the School of Public Health in Zagreb, Yugoslavia, recently stated that, when a country decided that industrialization was necessary, it should mobilize all its national forces to deal with the bad side effects—deficient nutrition, alcoholism, mental disorders, divorce, and juvenile delinquency.

The countries that need economic growth will have to develop a value-system that encourages both work and saving. The ideology that will be required to develop these virtues cannot be determined without a close examination of the existing views of the country, but it is certain that neither the pure capitalist nor the pure communist doctrines will be appropriate. All those who are concerned with helping the poor countries to develop must realize that the problems of each country are unique and solutions must be tailored to the real issues in the country. It will be insufficient merely to follow precedents; these can only act as guides and must not be considered as ideal patterns.

The poor countries will be forced to try to introduce new ideas and ideals more adequate for the new age they are entering. Some failures will be inevitable, but success will be more often achieved if the reasons for actions are understood—wrong diagnosis may lead to steps that will aggravate rather than improve the situation. For example, it has long been a common complaint among employers in the poor countries that native laborers were idle and would not work even if they were given good wages. It was therefore concluded that workers were irrational—this, incidentally, despite the existence of an economic theory that explained precisely the reasons for their behavior. If an individual prefers leisure to work, it is perfectly rational that he would do as little work as possible. An attempt to deal with a shortage of workers in this situation by raising wages—a rational action in the rich countries—might aggravate the problem under these circumstances.

The mere act of devising a policy intended to benefit those who will fall under its provisions is not necessarily enough to ensure that it will be welcomed or even accepted. The inhabitants of a country can perceive a proposal only in the light of their own values, and this will often result in misinterpretation of the situation—an adequate solution to a pressing problem may therefore be rejected. Such misunderstandings can occur quite independently of any desire to falsify the facts, although the existence of ill-faith will further increase the difficulty of adequate communication. The experience of an American researcher who settled in an Indian village soon after the American Government authorized its first large technical assistance program illustrates this. Although the American steadily denied that he was associated with the American technical aid program—and in fact was not—the Indians refused to believe him and were already "aware" of all the results of the program. They believed that it would involve taking over village houses, buying or seizing all the best land, and separating the children from their parents to send them away to school. Although they hoped that it would also result in an increase in the amount of food available, they were afraid they would be forced to accept food they did not like or, for religious reasons, should not eat.

This particular set of distortions may well seem absurd when examined by an outsider, but similar patterns of misunderstanding exist throughout the world between those with different sets of beliefs and values. An action intended to be beneficial will be closely examined and Machiavellian motives may be thought to exist even though they were remote from the ideas of the originators. It is therefore not enough to design an objectively satisfactory policy—it must also be "sold." Like all techniques, persuasion can be put to good or bad uses; its employment in the past to hypnotize nations must not blind us to the necessity of its use at the present time.

It is appropriate to conclude this section with an acknowledgment that many of the facts, arguments, and policies discussed here are understood and accepted by the politicians and leaders of the poor countries. In many cases where policies that act against the best interests of their countries have been adopted, it has been on the insistence of experts who claimed to understand their problems but who actually failed to see there that was an essential difference between the situations of the poor and the rich countries. The inhabitants of every country must make a major effort to understand the real problems in other parts of the world; they must not simply view them as an extension of their own difficulties.

Part II

THE RICH COUNTRIES

VII. *Growing Rich*

As we turn from examining the poverty of two thirds of the globe to the relative riches of the remainder, the most startling fact confronting us is that for the first time in history a proportion of the population of the world has been freed from the fear of famine. Any deficiencies in crops in one rich country can be made up by the purchase of surplus food from other areas. The majority of the people in the rich countries not only are able to buy the food and other commodities necessary for survival, they have funds left over after these basic purchases have been made. In the United States about a quarter of the money earned is not required for the purchase of "essentials" but can be spent as the individual desires; it is expected that this proportion will rise from a quarter to almost a half during the next decade. Although the standard of living is not so high at the present time in Europe, it has been rising more rapidly than in the United States since the war, and is expected to continue to move upward.

Despite the rapid rate of growth in all the rich countries poverty has not been abolished. There are certain areas where incomes are only a fraction of the national average because of a lack of employment opportunities and insufficient facilities for education. Economists have argued in the past that no government intervention was necessary to resolve these problems and that free enterprise would eventually raise incomes, but Gunnar Myrdal, in his book *The American Negro* and later in his studies of the problems of economic growth, suggested that this was unduly optimistic. He argued that there were self-perpetuating forces that would tend to keep the poor areas of the world poor and the distressed areas within a country distressed, while economic growth, once it had started, would cause developments making further growth easier. This mechanism can be illustrated by the fact that it is impossible in poverty-stricken areas to set aside the necessary resources that would allow an improvement in the educational standard and thus attract industry. Because business fails to move in and employment is not available, the most dynamic people will leave, as this will be the only way of obtaining opportunities commensurate with their abilities. The departure of the most ambitious and talented members of the community will still further depress its condition and make more difficult the task of improving it.

This vicious circle may be noted in other areas. If an urban district begins to decline, it sets in motion forces that hasten its decay. As the streets and houses become less well kept, the types of tenants previously attracted will go elsewhere and will be replaced by less desirable elements. As the process continues, the people who lived in the district when it was more respectable begin to move out. The level of rents that can be obtained will fall, and any efforts by local government authorities to arrest the decline will be gravely hampered by the low level of local taxes now obtainable. Man's self-interest will not always benefit the society; it may set up a train of forces that will worsen the general position of the community. It will sometimes be necessary for the government to intervene if the forces that prevent individuals from receiving education or cause slums in the urban areas are to be destroyed. While such actions have been recognized—in principle—as being in the general interest, there is still opposition from many, who argue that any tampering with free competition is wrong.

Despite the existence of pockets of poverty, the postwar years have seen a rapid increase in income. This, however, has not led to general satisfaction with the level of wages and salaries, for it has been accompanied by rising tastes. The "ideal" standard of living has remained out of reach—there continues to be products people want to buy and cannot afford. This has been true in America, where one of the signs of success has been "conspicuous consumption," although there is some evidence that the possession of an ever-increasing quantity of goods may be losing some of its appeal for those with the highest incomes in the United States. In Europe, on the other hand, an intense preoccupation with goods, either for their own sake or as a sign of status, was less typical in the past. There have, however, been unmistakable signs since the Second World War that the importance of a higher standard of living and a greater quantity of material goods is growing. There is disagreement about the strength of this trend, but there are few observers who do not expect an intensified desire for additional goods in the immediate future.

Little attention has been paid by economists to the forces causing people to adopt new tastes and purchase additional goods. This comparative neglect resulted from a generalized belief that wants were insatiable or that the problem was of little real importance, as it would never be possible to satisfy existing needs. Economics was dominated by the idea that the standard of living could not rise because of the pressure of increasing population. Only since the Second World War has a substantial number of the families of any country been able to pick and choose their purchases. Formerly a few very wealthy people obtained a very large proportion of the total income of the country; 1 per cent of the income receivers in America got 17 per cent of the national income in 1929. Now a large part of the population can buy luxuries. When wealth was highly concentrated, its existence was evidenced by ostentation and by the employment of numbers of servants; at the present time it is difficult to find satisfactory domestic help and display is distrusted. The patterns of expenditure adopted in the future will not simply be modeled on the past, they must be expected to be very different.

What causes a person to spend his money? Expenditure must almost always involve some dissatisfaction, for supplies of money are limited. If it is not spent in one way it can be used in another or may be saved to provide security against an emergency. It must therefore be felt that the satisfaction obtained from purchasing a product will be greater than the dissatisfaction of paying for it. People will be most concerned about spending money if their income is insufficient to provide for their needs; if they have more than enough money, they will worry less.

The purchase and possession of a product or service will be considered worth while if it provides either services or prestige or both. The product may satisfy a man's hunger, prevent him from being uncomfortably hot or cold, protect him from, or cure him, of disease, amuse him, or satisfy his aesthetic tastes. The valuation placed on each of these services by different people will vary. An article may also be considered valuable because its possession will confer prestige, or its purchase may be avoided because it would unfavorably affect status. Prestige may be attached to almost all purchases because they provide general evidence of success or may be concentrated on certain items.

The distinction between the services rendered by a product and the prestige to be obtained from its possession is not clear-cut. Hunger is satisfied in different ways in various cultures; societies find their amusement in many forms. The Italian, whose main dishes are *pasta,* finds the Indian's curries strange; Eastern forms of music are not generally appreciated in the West. The services rendered by an article and the prestige it confers are inextricably mixed; people do not buy a thousand calories of food, they purchase strawberries for a special dinner because they have come to regard them as a luxury.

The fact that prestige is attached to certain goods is not a new phenomenon, it has probably existed in all societies. Even groups that attached little importance to wealth required the possession of certain articles; if the individual did not own them he would be shamed. While the objective services rendered by such objects were sometimes also important, it was their symbolic value—confirming the position of the person in society—that was vital. The phenomenon also occurs at the present time: when the possession of a television set was becoming part of the working-class standard of living in England after the war, the demand for aerials to be erected on the roofs of private houses as a visible sign of possession ran far ahead of actual purchases of television sets for an extended period. The need to claim ownership was strong enough to justify useless expenditure.

The manufacturer can therefore raise the apparent value of his products to the consumer in two different ways. First, he can increase the service his products will render. In order to attain this goal, manufacturers in America have been willing to multiply their expenditure on research and development seventy-five times during the last forty years. Second, the firm can also try to increase the prestige associated with the articles it sells, attempting to influence the customer to feel that he is neither successful nor secure unless he purchases certain products. The attempt to change the prestige associated with certain goods almost certainly has far more limited effects than advertising agencies would have us believe, and the reason is clear. As noted, each person requires that the satisfaction he receives from a purchase should be enough to compensate him for the dissatisfaction of spending the money he possesses. Advertising cannot compensate for failure to provide the required services and therefore cannot ensure a continuing sale for inferior products. Advertising has been unsuccessful in changing basic trends, even the heavy campaigns to promote the sale of beer have not arrested the long-run decline in its total consumption.

In his book *The Affluent Society,* Professor Galbraith suggested that at the same time new goods were introduced the manufacturers persuaded the customer that he needed them, that in the United States the genuine tastes of the inhabitants were already satisfied. Leaving aside the existence of poverty-stricken families and of large numbers who have insufficient incomes without being actually poverty-stricken, this analysis is too simple. Families are willing to buy additional goods, partly because new goods are always being introduced that make life easier or more amusing, partly because increasing wealth increases the resources available for making purchases and partly because the United States attaches great importance to consumption levels as an index of prestige.

The free enterprise system is still working in the main to

produce goods the consumer believes are worth buying.
While advertising does enhance the value of the goods purchased, the consumer normally buys because he believes that
the product will either make life easier or increase prestige.
When prestige is associated with purchases, it has normally
been developed by society as a whole rather than through
the efforts of the advertising industry. If people are attracted
by newness and novelty, the introduction of additional products will be accepted by society. If, on the other hand, goods
are considered a nuisance, the objective services rendered by
the product will have to be very obvious before purchases
are made. Major changes in buying habits will occur when
there is an alteration in the attitude toward goods, and this
will be caused by social trends rather than by advertising
ballyhoo.

The desire for consumption in the rich countries encourages people to work longer hours than would be necessary if
tastes were more modest; indeed work itself has been made
part of the ethos of the rich countries. Leisure is somehow
vaguely wrong. Most people in the rich countries would not
choose a life without any form of work even if they would
receive the same amount of money for doing nothing as for
working; if a man did prefer leisure his wife might veto
the suggestion. The number of hours men would choose to
work might be lower than those customary at the present
time, but they would be unhappy confronted with the prospect of years of idleness.

The relative importance of work and leisure will vary in
the rich countries; the rate at which they have chosen, and
will elect, to take extra leisure rather than consumption
depends on the values of the country. It is probable that
Americans, Scandinavians, and Germans have the greatest
respect for work as a way of life, a suggestion verified both
by observation and their rate of growth in the past. Since

the war England and France have attached increasing importance to work, while there is some evidence that the value placed on effort in America is now declining.

The importance attached to work and to success in business in the rich countries has led many individuals to construct their whole lives around the firms in which they are employed. In the nineteenth century many did so because they believed in the Protestant ethic of hard work and saving. In the twentieth century many find their jobs most important because it is in them that they can gain the power, prestige, and money they desire. Others find their work more fascinating than any "leisure" activity. As most of the managerial and entrepreneurial classes in the rich countries find work important, either because of its intrinsic interest or fascination or because it is the way to achieve the prestige they desire, success often does not reduce the amount of work done but augments it—promotion will normally bring an increase in responsibilities. People work to raise the profits of their firms; it is in this way their talents will be recognized and they can attain the desired success.

This explains why increasing levels of taxation, the greater responsibilities governments have assumed in taking care of the individual if he is unable to find a job or falls sick, and the increasing interference of the government in the economy have not caused the decline in the rate of economic growth that was sometimes predicted. Economists argued that if people were unable to obtain such large monetary rewards from their work, or were freed from the danger of starvation if they failed to find employment, it was to be expected that the amount of effort would fall substantially. This has now been shown to be untrue; social attitudes *require* work in the rich countries; the idler is frowned upon. Here again, as in the case of consumption, only changes in social attitudes will substantially alter the actions of people; economic factors are of relatively little importance.

The object of a firm during the nineteenth century was normally to make as large a profit as was possible. The economic theory of the normal behavior of the firm developed during this period claimed—and usually correctly so—that the aim of the owner of the firm was to buy his supplies (including his workers) as cheaply as possible, and to sell the goods he made as expensively as possible. But as the firm ceased to be ruled by one man and came to be controlled by a salaried management staff, it developed a corporate ethos whose aim can no longer be so simply expressed. The first duty is probably to ensure that the firm should continue to exist and the second to make a "proper" profit; the manager is expected to *balance* the interests of the stockholders, labor, customers, and suppliers. He is thought to have a duty toward each of these groups and it is considered that the firm can be successful only when the interests of all of them have been taken into account. While some firms do not accept this aim in its totality, almost all important enterprises now believe that their object must be something more than to function as a mere profit-making machine.

The change in the attitude of the enterprise to its responsibilities appears to be leading to a major challenge in labor-management relations. In the early days of labor unions, management and labor were inherently hostile; it was management's job to keep as much of the profits as possible for the shareholder, it was labor's task to obtain for its members as large an increase in wages and other benefits as possible. This conflict declined with the acceptance of labor's right to share in the benefits of increasing productivity and, since the end of the war, unions and management have often "combined" to allow wage increases. These were often followed by rising prices and inflation. In recent years, however, General Electric has pioneered a policy that is spreading in the United States—each firm has a responsibility to *all* those with whom it is associated (stockholders, labor, suppliers, customers) and it is therefore the duty of management alone to decide how profits from the operations of the enterprise should be distributed. Such a philosophy is clearly anathema to the unions, for they envisage the process of wage-fixing as one of bargaining between management, which looks after the interests of the stockholders, and the unions, which look after the interests of labor. Two philosophies therefore come into conflict: the one, which suggests that management has the right and the duty to make decisions about the distribution of the profits of the firm, particularly the amount labor should receive; the other, which believes that the unions have a right to a voice in these affairs and that the decisions of management are not final but subject to negotiation.

This challenge to the power of unions may lead to greater alterations in the concept of labor negotiations than any other development in the last thirty years. The new theory of management, if carried to its logical conclusion, requires the manager to look after the legitimate interests of the worker and excludes the union from this process. This philosophy has enabled General Electric to reduce greatly the power of the unions in its plants by granting advantages that are different from those suggested or demanded by the unions but that receive the approval of the individual worker.

The problems that may be caused by this development were exemplified by the 1959 steel strike in America. The steel firms started bargaining with a fixed determination not to allow any wage increases on the grounds that this would be inflationary, and later demanded greater control over working rules. The unions challenged these decisions, stating that the companies could afford to increase wages without increasing prices, that wage increases would therefore cause no inflationary pressure, while the work rules protected the labor force from any unreasonable speeding up in rates of work. The longest steel strike in history resulted.

The difficulty of arbitrating the issues was clearly shown by an exchange in one of President Eisenhower's press conferences a short time before the strike started. He was asked whether he would favor the administration setting out the "facts" in the steel dispute and he replied that this would appear to be a good idea. The administration, however, promptly turned down the suggestion, claiming that figures of wages, profits, productivity, etc., could not be presented without bias.

A more important problem, however, is the need to find appropriate rules for the distribution of increasing wealth. None of the relationships valid in the past can be used, for changing conditions have made them unsatisfactory. Thus, when the increasing pressure to settle the steel strike forced the administration to issue the figures it had previously wished to withhold, they scarcely affected the issue. Both labor and management claimed that the official information supported their stands, labor justifying a demand for higher wages and management a refusal to pay on the basis of the same figures.

Relationships among the "right" level of wages, salaries, and profits will be still further changed in future years by the growth of automation and the installation of computer-guided operations. Does automation increase the amount of skill required and therefore decrease boredom, or does it increase the responsibility of the operator to such an extent that he becomes worried and unhappy? Should automation result in higher pay for those placed on jobs of this type or should the gain be spread throughout the factory or the

economy as a whole? Can layoffs be avoided by gradual installation of automated equipment or by the transfer of those displaced *within* the factory? Will the number of individuals who have have to be downgraded because of an inability to deal with the new complexities in manufacturing be large or small?

The future impact of automation is still greatly underestimated. Despite the increase in the production of goods in the United States in recent years, there is now a smaller manual labor force than in the immediate postwar period, although a parallel increase in the number of white-collar workers has kept the total number employed in manufacturing from declining greatly. The decrease in the number of manual jobs that can be anticipated will make it essential that those who would have taken them are enabled either to find white-collar jobs or to move into the service sector of the economy.

Automation can be expected to modify accepted ideas radically. For it to be profitable, machinery must not be stopped either for lack of raw materials or because of breakdowns; the failure of one part of an automated production line often means that the whole process will be out of action. The growth of the need for absolute reliability in supplies of raw materials and other goods has led management in the past to try to obtain greater control over their sources of supply, and this trend can be expected to continue in future years. It will also result in a lessened insistence on the absolute minimal cost of production and a greater demand for efficiency and reliability in manufacture; the reduction in expenses attainable by purchasing at the lowest price will seldom compensate for the additional expenditure incurred either by a complete failure in supply or by unsatisfactory quality.

Automation will increase the cost of any failure in selling,

and the results of this failure will be more serious for the profits of the enterprise. In the past the impact of a downturn in sales could at least be mitigated by laying off workers as sales declined; in the future labor costs will in many cases be only a relatively small part of total expenses, while the need to pay depreciation on capital goods and interest on money cannot be avoided but only postponed if the enterprise is to remain in business. This increased pressure to sell might lead to new methods; for example, it might be worth while for the manufacturer of a television set not to sell it outright but to rent its services. It would be installed and serviced by the company. The periodic replacement of the sets after a stated period of years would give the enterprise an assured market for its production.

The very high cost of automated machinery and the closer ties between firms that will be required in the future will certainly increase the importance of "big business." The growing complexity of the economy and the impact of business firms' decisions on the welfare of the inhabitants of the various rich countries has made increasing government control essential over various facets of business activity. The relationships between governments and business will certainly become closer, although it is still uncertain whether they will be co-operative or whether governments will exert ever-closer control over industry.

At this point certain economists and social observers exclaim in horror at the evolution pictured—big business will increase in importance, while its power may be expected to be enhanced by automation. They argue that any such development must be opposed since it interferes with the ideal of many small businesses, in which the owner-manager can develop his full potential. It is, however, far from proved that the existence of the large firm is sufficient to prevent the emergence and eventual success of the small enterprise.

Indeed, many believe that the large firm is inherently at a disadvantage in competing in new fields, for it fails to take decisions rapidly enough. Thus many inventions on the boundaries of knowledge have come from the small firm rather than from the large laboratories. This is particularly obvious in the case of such new industries as electronics.

The basic response to any suggestion that the increasing importance of the large firm should be curtailed is that its destruction would tear down the foundation on which economic growth in the rich countries has been built. This may not have been the only possible pattern that could have achieved this result, but it cannot now be reversed. What, then, are the reasons for the generalized distrust of the large firm? It stems to a great extent from the enterprises in the nineteenth and early twentieth centuries, when entrepreneurs tried to maximize profits regardless of the effects of their actions on the community. This attitude is no longer prevalent; the responsibility of the enterprise to the society in which it is placed is generally accepted. A second reason for the distrust stems from the theories, developed by economists during the 1930's, that "proved" that monopolies and large companies would produce a lesser output at a higher price than would result if all firms were small.

This theory is no longer valid, for it is based on neoclassical assumptions; first, that all firms are trying to maximize their profits and, second, that all enterprises have perfect knowledge of the markets, products, techniques, etc., required for efficient operation. This ignores the fact that probably the most important factor in economic growth today is expenditure on research and development. It is *only* by using these inaccurate assumptions that it is possible to prove that the smaller firm will produce more at a cheaper rate than the large firm. The existence of big business will not *normally* result in a restriction of output; this will only occur in isolated instances where firms take specific steps to raise prices or limit output.

The policy of certain governments toward big business, notably that of the United States, needs to be changed. It has often seemed to contain a suggestion that bigness and success in a branch of business are prima-facie evidence of improper practices. In the future, as in the past, bigness will be one of the facts of the industrial scene. It will therefore be unwise for governments to launch suits simply because a firm is large and successful. It must be proved that its policies have increased the cost of a product or diminished the amount of goods produced or in some other way unfavorably affected the general interest.

In this chapter, we have seen that the rich countries, and especially America, have become affluent in the years since the war. We will examine in the next the factors that have caused the inflation in the rich countries, suggesting that changes in social attitudes will be required if it is to be overcome.

VIII. *Is Inflation a Greater Danger than a Slump?*

AT THE END of the Second World War, economists concentrated their attention on methods of avoiding the catastrophic slump that was expected throughout the world. However, such downturns in business activity as did occur were relatively easily controlled. The success in avoiding depressions was not paralleled in the field of price control—prices rose in all countries of the world during this period. As a result the emphasis in economic policy began to pass from the necessity of ensuring that all the resources of the economy were used and unemployment avoided to a concern with inflation. This change did not occur at the same time in all countries. Perhaps the first government to take really serious measures against inflation and overfull employment was England. However, as world-wide inflation continued and as depressions continued to have relatively minor effects on the economies of the rich countries—

although their indirect effects in the poor countries have often been severe—the attention of economists has turned more and more to the effects of inflation and the methods that could be used to avoid it. Considerable business and political pressure has built up in the same area.

Economists are unable to agree at the present time on the reasons for inflation, on the steps that might be taken to limit its pace or abolish it altogether, or even on whether stable prices can be achieved without a serious slump. Some argue that economic growth is most important and that a slow rise in prices is not an unduly heavy price to pay in order to attain it; others suggest that stable prices are so vital that all necessary steps must be taken to ensure them. One camp argues that in present conditions vital economic growth can be attained only at the cost of some inflation, others that the effects of inflation are so pernicious that even a depression can be tolerated if this is the only way of controlling it. This chapter discusses the reasons why inflation occurs, its effects, and the way in which it can be controlled.

The first problem is how to decide whether inflation—that is, a rise in prices and a fall in the value of money—is in fact taking place. It would appear from the considerable uproar that follows a rise of only a few tenths of 1 per cent in the consumers' price index that the methods of measuring the level of prices must be completely accurate. In reality, these indices are not very satisfactory. No adequate way has been found, for example, of taking account of the fact that the product sold under the same name from year to year often incorporates substantial improvements in design and product life, or that in some cases its durability has been deliberately reduced. The articles included in the index usually lag behind changes in the pattern of consumer purchases—for example, it is only in recent years that candles were removed from the British cost-of-living index. In addition, the effect of alterations in prices will be very different, depending on purchasing patterns. For example, families that buy predominantly food and manufactured goods will normally have suffered far less from the rise in prices than those renting houses or apartments and paying large sums for services—doctor's bills, amusement, travel, etc.

The continuing inflation since the Second World War followed the acceptance of a new social theory that held that the worker should benefit from increases in productivity. The first agreement of this type between General Motors and the United Automobile Workers agreed that the automobile worker should receive a percentage wage increase each year roughly equivalent to the rate of increase of productivity within the industry. Additional increases in wages were to be given if they were necessary to offset changes in the cost of living. The whole concept of the importance of rising productivity and the social justice of allowing the worker to share in the fruits of any increases was rapidly taken up in Europe and later in the poor countries under the impact of the technical-assistance programs set up by the United States.

It was not realized when this new social attitude was adopted that its results would almost inevitably be inflationary. Increases in productivity in the various sectors of the economy—agriculture, manufacturing, and the service sectors—are usually at different rates. In the past, increases in manufacturing productivity have been most rapid; in recent years the application of modern technology has led to a very rapid increase in agricultural productivity. In the service sectors increases in productivity have inevitably lagged; efficiency will probably continue to rise at a slower pace, for the scope for mechanization is far more limited. It has been estimated, for example, that the rate of increase in American manufacturing productivity has been twice as great as in distribution in recent years.

It would be unreasonable and unrealistic to expect workers in the service sectors of the economy to allow their wages to fall further and further behind those in manufacturing. They will demand higher wages and better working conditions in order to offset the gains made by those in manufacturing industries and will strike if they are unable to obtain them. The higher wages and benefits coupled with a limited rise in productivity results in an increase in prices. Changes in manufacturing wages inevitably affect incomes in other parts of the economy: a sensible wage policy cannot be developed in isolation.

Economists have therefore been asked with increasing frequency in recent years what would be the "right" distribution of the available wealth in a country. What relation should the wages of a coal miner, a steelworker, a white-collar worker, and the chief justice of any country have to each other? How large a profit should firms make? Under what circumstances should a rise in profits lead to a rise in wages and when should there be a decrease in prices? In part, these questions are unanswerable by "economists," for they demand judgments about the right course of actions, a field in which the values and beliefs of each person affect their decisions. Is it right for the president of a company to receive a far larger salary than the worker who produces the articles? Failure to answer this question is not caused by the inadequacy of the economist but lies in the nature of the problem. Nevertheless, economic theory is partly at fault, for it has not produced tools to make it possible to examine the problem meaningfully. It is no longer enough to say that free competition will result in the best distribution of resources, for prices are not primarily set by supply and demand and wages are influenced by collective bargaining.

The tools developed in the 1930's of imperfect or monopolistic competition are equally useless, for they assume that a firm has all the information required for efficient operation; while one of the most important—if not the most vital force—in securing growth at the present time is the development of new knowledge through research. It is therefore necessary to re-examine the fundamental forces that should determine wages, prices, and profits. We will find, however, that the distribution of wealth cannot be entirely determined by the feeling of the community about what is "right." Certain changes will be necessary if supply and demand are to be kept in balance and depressions avoided.

It will not be easy to determine the best distribution of wealth in a society, and it is probable that it will never be possible to produce more than aids to understanding in this field. It is now generally agreed that the object of a firm must be to produce goods at a price people are willing to pay, while giving "reasonable wages" to its employees, a "reasonable return" to the stockholders, and insuring a "reasonable rate of growth"—using either its own profits or by borrowing money from investors. Each of these claims must be met if the firm is to continue to operate; the problem is that each "reasonable" in the above statement conceals a wide range of attitudes about the "right" course of action.

The difficulties in deciding on the right distribution of wealth are further increased by changes in economic organization and social attitudes. The proper relationships between wages and prices, profits and dividends are constantly altering, so that those attitudes appropriate and acceptable in a previous period are no longer satisfactory. For example, the postwar years have seen an increase in the proportion of investment expenditures financed by retained profits rather than by further borrowing. The level of profits required by a firm is therefore higher than in earlier periods. The right level of profits also depends on the amount of investment the firm will need to carry out in the future. The profits of a firm in an expanding industry will normally be higher than those in a stagnant or declining one, both because the firm's ability to earn profits is greater and its need more urgent if it is to obtain the money required for expansion.

The major change in social attitudes toward the distribution of national income in the years since the war followed the acknowledgment of the right of the worker to share fully in the benefits from increases in efficiency in his firm. The differing economic conditions in the rich countries governed the effects of this change. At the end of the war America suffered from a shortage of goods, as did all the rich countries, but her wealth, coupled with unparalleled productive capacity, ensured that supply soon caught up with demand. The date at which this occurred was delayed by the Korean War and subsequent stockpiling, but by 1953 supply and demand were in approximate balance. The main force leading to price increases since this date was not shortages of goods but wage increases in industries and service sectors of the economy where productivity was rising too slowly to offset the increase in labor costs.

In Europe demand was greater than supply until the latter part of the 1950's; this difference in experience compared to the United States was largely caused by varying social philosophies. Most European countries introduced a very high level of taxation during the war and this was continued after hostilities ended—in England the state takes over 80 per cent of all incomes over £10,000 ($28,000). As individuals' post-tax incomes were reduced, the amount of money that was saved declined; many felt the level of taxation was so high they could not afford to save, and some decided that they also should spend their previous savings, as most of the money they possessed would pass to the state at their death. Governments, however, spent larger sums of money than before, partly to meet new social obligations and partly on armaments. Industry needed to replace the equipment that had worn out during the war. The result was that total demand for goods in all European countries was greater than could be met.

The differing experience of three European countries since the war will illustrate some important factors. At the end of the war West German industry ground to an almost complete halt. Development appeared impossible and it was not until the currency reform of 1948 cut the value of the mark substantially that production increased. Because of the reduction in the value of money, the funds available in the economy were limited and consumer goods could be purchased only by those willing and able to work; supply and demand were in approximate balance. As progress continued and the amount of unemployment declined, the unions proved willing to postpone wage increases, accepting the proclaimed doctrine that the recovery of Germany and an increase in her productive capacity were more important than increases in individual incomes. Large sums were plowed back into the expansion of production and prices stayed low—so low indeed that the availability of German goods at prices substantially under those of other European countries caused a crisis in the structure of European payments. The German recovery was also helped by the fact that few resources were used in the production of weapons.

France came out of the war with a grossly inflated currency—individuals had hoarded large sums of money. Although the danger of allowing this money to be used to purchase goods in short supply was appreciated, no action was taken. As a result France suffered from fairly rapid inflation over the postwar period—only short breaks in the upward movement of prices took place. The imbalance of supply and demand was increased by the practically continuous involvement of the French Army in colonial wars. The French balance of payments was in substantial deficit, more goods being imported than exported; and without foreign loans, extended largely by the United States, the French economy would have found it difficult to survive. Despite this inflation, the rates of investment and growth were high during the 1950's—higher than at any previous period in French history. It was not until 1958 that a major attempt was made to cure the weakness of the French economy.

In England the shortage of goods during the war, coupled with strict control of purchases and the willingness of the population to save to ensure victory, resulted in the existence of a large volume of savings at the end of the war. People wished and felt entitled to spend freely after years of austerity. The surplus of money, compared to the amount of available goods, was increased by the payment of fairly substantial sums as discharge gratuities to servicemen. Prices soared; excessive demand for foreign goods forced the continuation of import controls, which in turn, led to continued restrictions. The period of greatest hardship for the British people came after the war ended—rationing continued into 1954. When the Conservatives came to power early in the 1950's, they decided that the only way to achieve a reduction of inflationary pressure was to limit the money supply by increases in the rate of interest and direct credit controls. Their success would have been greater if the workers had not become accustomed to annual wage increases during the period of rapidly rising prices in the late 1940's, and were unwilling to forego them in order to reduce inflationary pressures. As a result of these restrictions on credit, the rate of investment and the rate of growth in Great Britain have been considerably lower than in Germany or France during the 1950's.

The comparison of the experiences of America, England, France, and Germany points up several economic relationships. The use of credit controls to restrict inflation will not be successful if the basic cause of the rise in prices is pressure for increased wages; these policies have little effect on the demands of unions for wage increases or the amount granted by management following their claims. A marked alteration could be secured only by causing a major slump, with heavy unemployment, and this policy is now considered unsatisfactory. Inflation *will* be limited when it is realized that the accepted doctrine of sharing productivity increases with the workers and keeping prices stable in industries with rapidly rising productivity *must* lead to over-all inflation. It seems probable that this lesson cannot be imposed on labor by management; it must be demonstrated.

Credit control will limit the rate of economic growth, for it will cut into the amount of money available for investment. The rate of growth in Britain, where credit control continued throughout the 1950's, was far slower than occurred in France, and the greater French rate of growth was obtained despite inflation. The unfavorable effects of credit control on growth could be partially avoided if only consumer credit could be restricted, but the mechanisms to ensure this result are not available. However, an excess of demand over supply and inflation can be allowed to continue only if the country concerned does not have to worry about the consequent imbalance between imports and exports. For the result of an unsatisfied demand for goods will be that merchants will attempt to buy more food from abroad while manufacturers will be less willing to search out overseas markets. Exports will normally be smaller than imports and the country will find that its reserves of foreign currency will decline. Such a policy will therefore be possible only if another country is willing to underwrite the export deficit. In the 1950's the United States did this for France; the United Kingdom, on the other hand, was unwilling to rely on outside aid. We will return to this subject in the last part of the book, showing that many poor countries will be unable to obtain growth without an excess of demand over supply and will therefore run a balance of payments deficit. It will be argued that the rich countries must devise means to prevent this deficit from inhibiting economic growth.

As economic actions will be effective in controlling only the type of inflation that is caused by wage increases if they are allowed to bring on a major slump, we must examine the dangers of rising prices and be able to compare them with the impact of a large amount of unemployment. The effects of a slow rate of inflation are not so serious as they have often been claimed to be. In some cases there has been considerable distortion of the facts in so-called educational advertising; the idea was conveyed that inflation actually decreases the amount of production. The statement that inflation has destroyed 50 per cent of the value of a currency has often been used to give the impression that production would have been twice as large if there had been no inflation. The value of money, however, is only a convenience; if the quantity of real resources each person controls remains the same, it does not matter directly if the amount of money that has to be paid for the goods doubles.

Inflation affects the distribution of income and wealth in three major ways: by changing wage rates, by affecting the value of savings, and by altering the amount of money available in certain sectors of the economy—government and the private sector, management and labor, etc. In each case judgment about the effects of inflation will depend on ideas about the right distribution of resources. The result of rising prices in most rich countries has been an increase in the amount of money received by workers and a decrease in the sums obtained by those with fixed incomes and by families in the upper- and middle-income brackets. Even when those with higher incomes have been able to obtain the same percentage increase in gross income as those with lower wages—and this has not normally been the case—their rise in income will move them into a higher tax bracket and increase the percentage paid in taxes. In addition, there is some evidence that the effect of inflation has been to make it possible for those unions with the greatest power to obtain the largest increases in wages, leaving the less-well-organized and the unorganized worker behind. Judgment of these effects will depend on the attitude of the person examining them. It seems probable that the trend toward greater equality would be found acceptable by most, that decreases in the resources of those with fixed incomes—particularly those living on pensions—would be judged unfavorable, and that the evaluation of changes in relative wage rates would depend on the point of view.

The second issue raised by inflation is the way it affects savings. It reduces their value below that which would have been attained if inflation had not taken place. This does not necessarily mean that the value of the money returned will be less than that invested; if the rate of inflation is lower than the rate of interest, the individual will still be able to purchase a greater amount of goods than would have been possible if he had used the money immediately; it is only if the rate of inflation is higher than the rate of interest that the individual would be actually worse off because he saved rather than spent his money. Nevertheless, it is often held that inflation violates an implied pledge that the value of money will remain unchanged. But others have argued that the payment of interest is essentially a convention—one that through the ages has probably gained more moral obloquy than any other part of capitalism.

Once the moral issue, rather than the effect on the economy, has been introduced, it can be cogently argued that fairness to the saver would lie not in keeping prices stable, but in allowing all the benefit from increasing productivity to be passed on to society as a whole in the form of lower prices. The firm would not benefit from its efforts directly; all the gains would be distributed throughout the community. The saver would benefit from the decline in prices, he would receive a far larger quantity of goods when he chose to spend his savings than he would have been able to purchase if he had used the money immediately. Although the mechanism outlined above might constitute abstract social justice, there are few economists who suggest that this policy should be followed. It is generally agreed that continually falling prices would act as a drag on business, while the requirement that the firm should not benefit directly from its innovations might well cut the amount of effort willingly expended in introducing new goods.

It is often assumed that all savings are affected by inflation; in actual fact many forms of savings are protected from its effects. At the present time a large part of the savings in the rich countries is made by businesses that are largely protected from inflation. Another large part results from the high incomes of wealthy individuals, although heavy tax rates have cut their savings, particularly in Europe. The greater part of savings by the rich is merely a result of the fact that the person's income is larger than is required to meet immediate needs. He makes no sacrifice—or only a very minor one—in not spending money, for he has already bought all the goods and services he wants to buy. In a very real sense it would be more difficult to spend the money than to save it. One type of person, however, *is* likely to suffer from inflation—the small saver who is unable to obtain the advice that would allow him to avoid its unfavorable effects.

A potentially more serious result of inflation is undoubtedly its effect on the amount of money available in certain sectors of the economy. Inflation has tended to increase the difficulties of governments in securing money to provide essential services. It is, however, doubtful if the basic difficulty stems from inflation; the most important factors are that social and technological conditions are changing, necessitating government control of a larger part of the economy. This is coupled with the fact that citizens are traditionally unenthusiastic about taxation, despite the fact that they value the services it makes possible; while in some countries, particularly in America, there is a congenital distrust of all government action. Although the absence of inflation might slightly reduce the difficulty of governments in securing sufficient revenue, it is certain that the main problems will continue as long as huge sums are required for armaments and the individual views taxes only as a burden. It will be necessary for him to look beyond the money he pays to the services taxation makes possible. Until this is achieved it seems unlikely that the conflict between the government's need for more money and the individual's ideas about the distribution of his income will cease.

To summarize briefly: Inflation has serious effects on certain classes in society—those living on pensions and with small savings; it also acts to distort the social balance. However, inflation caused by increasing wages can be arrested only by a change in attitudes or a major slump; the former will take time, the latter would be far more costly in terms of welfare. Growth and inflation *can* occur together; the unfavorable effects of inflation are limited by the favorable effects of growth. However, a slump causes considerable unfavorable changes in the distribution of income and *also* an over-all decline in incomes. Inflation is clearly less unfavorable so long as its rates are moderate—those particularly affected can be protected by special measures. The distrust of inflation is largely based on neoclassical assumptions—that free competition will result in the fairest possible division of the national income, inflation's interference with this division *must* be bad. But these assumptions are invalid; inflation may actually improve the distribution of wealth in certain cases.

If the social damage caused by inflation is relatively minor and if it actually tends to improve the position of workers in the most powerful unions, why did a large proportion of the American steelworkers feel that a wage increase in 1959 would not improve their position—that the benefits from the rise in wages would be canceled by inflation. This view was caused by a combination of circumstances, but three major factors can be distinguished. First, some "educational advertising" suggests that inflation can cut production and the rate of growth—a result that can only occur with a far faster rate of inflation than has taken place in the United States in the 1950's. Second, the prices of goods are always changing, some up and some down—if inflation is considered a threat it is not surprising that only the increases are remembered. The average rate of increase in real income is only 2 or 3 per cent per year on the average, it may easily appear that all this is being taken up by price increases.

Third, and probably most important, is the continued increase in desired or enforced government expenditure. For example, communities require more schools to accommodate the increasing number of children and they have not been satisfied with the old standards. This has required larger payments from the residents of the community, and in many cases it has proved convenient to blame inflation for the increased costs. The reaction against inflation is certainly based to a large extent on the hope that if it is arrested all tax increases will cease. This hope is foredoomed, for it is precisely in the service area, where most government expenditure is concentrated, that increases in efficiency can least easily be obtained, and where a further augmentation of expenditure will be required if the social balance is to be maintained.

The recent concentration on the problems of inflation has considerable dangers. Labor-management relations may be expected to deteriorate if management is determined to assert its control over profits and wages in the name of an anti-inflationary campaign without convincing labor of the need for smaller wage increases. But the crucial problem lies elsewhere. Each year an increased amount of goods is produced by the rich countries, and they must be purchased if a slump is not to result. Concentration on avoiding inflation may result in the far graver danger of there being an insufficient demand for goods. In addition, the fear of inflation in America has caused the government to refuse to accept responsibility in areas where only *its* actions could be effective—on the ground that this would unbalance the budget. The need to abolish substandard housing and to build educational facilities is urgent; it cannot be sidestepped because of an outworn financial shibboleth. The most important economic rule is that the demand for goods should remain in approximate balance with the possible supply.

IX. *Constructive Spending*

IT WAS JOHN MAYNARD KEYNES who first developed the idea that supply and demand might get out of balance in an economy; although his ideas were rejected at first by economists, they soon came to be accepted. It was the use of Keynesian theory that led many economists to predict a serious slump at the end of the Second World. Its failure to develop and the successful maintenance of relatively full employment since the end of the war in the rich countries have tended to cast some doubts on the validity of his concepts. However, his basic theory is incontrovertible. A depression will occur when the demand for goods is insufficient to balance the amount supplied. The tendency toward a slump is increased when those with available resources do not use them—for example, when people save money instead of spending it; it is decreased when people spend more and save less.

What developments changed the picture Keynes drew in the 1930's of the future of the rich countries, and prevented the slumps and semi-permanent unemployment he predicted? His book was written before the recent burst of innovation; he therefore believed that the tastes of people could be assumed to be fixed for purposes of analysis. In actual fact, the 1940's and 1950's have seen a revolution in the accepted and desired standard of living. The result of the rising level of tastes has been to increase the amount of income a person must earn before he "feels" that he can afford to save. The effect of this rise in the amount of goods each family feels it needs has been reinforced by the increasing number of children in most of the rich countries; each wage earner has, on the average, a larger number of people to support and the possibility of saving is therefore further decreased.

A second factor that helped to avoid the postwar depression that would have been expected on the basis of Keynesian analysis has been the increase in government expenditures. A far larger part of the resources of each country is used by government now than before the war. This is not a mere transfer of expenditure: many goods, particularly weapons, now manufactured for the government were not produced at all or made in far smaller quantities before the war, while many governments have also accepted new social responsibilities. The favorable effect on demand of this development is reinforced by the fact that taxation is progressive— the richest members of society pay a larger proportion of their income to the state than the poor. In America, where after-tax incomes are highest, the income received by the richest 1 per cent of the population had fallen from 17 per cent of the total in 1929 to 9 per cent in 1948. The result of this trend toward equality in incomes in these countries is to reduce individual savings. When rich people receive more money than they spend; the surplus money is saved or used to buy stocks simply because it is not spent. On the other hand, the amount of money put aside because the individual feels that he would like or ought to save is usually far smaller; the apparent urgency of consumption requirements makes it difficult to save money, even though there should be a genuine desire to do so. The result of heavy taxation on those with high incomes is to cut down their incomes and therefore to reduce savings.

These trends have acted to increase the amount of money spent rather than saved out of a given income, and thus the amount of goods purchased. There is one additional factor that has helped to control depressions, and that is a better understanding of their development. In the past almost any firm confronted with a decrease in the demand for its products not only heavily reduced its current production but also put off any plans for expansion. This helped to deepen the slump, for those firms that would have supplied the goods needed by the enterprise found their orders declining; this in turn reduced their current production and the orders they normally gave—depressions snowballed. Many firms are now coming to realize that if the general trend of demand for their product is upward, the best possible moment to expand may often be during a depression, when they are able to obtain special prices for the equipment they want to buy, and the rate of interest charged for money will also be low.

It would not be inaccurate to describe as revolutionary the changes that have combined to avoid depressions; however, many of them came about because of the need for additional government spending during the war years rather than as deliberate measures to avoid depressions. Tax rates equivalent to those now applied could never have been imposed except in a period of national emergency, and there are still politicians who hope that they will be reduced. The British

National Health Service would probably not have come into existence if the necessary taxation had not already been levied; the decrease in armaments expenditure made it possible to set up the service without any increase in tax payments. In order to ensure an adequate demand for available production in the next decades, further changes in social views will be required; these will be possible only if there is greater understanding of the economy and more willingness to examine the facts rather than to react on the basis of pre-existing theories. We will require the progressive abandonment of slogans and an increasing preoccupation with the desire to do the best possible job in the changing circumstances.

What then of the future? We can concentrate on the problems and prospects of America, for the other rich countries desire to attain the standard of living of the United States. It seems probable that while American consumption continues to increase the other rich countries will have relatively little difficulty in finding an outlet for all the goods they can manufacture. In order to understand the problem in America's economic future, we must re-examine why it exists. There has been no period in the history of the United States when there has not been a potential demand for all the goods that could have been produced; the difficulty was that those who desired the goods could not make their demand effective for lack of cash or credit. The great depression of the 1930's was caused by the failure of the United States and the other rich countries to put money in the hands of those who would have been willing to spend it. In the next decades the problem will be the same, to ensure that sufficient income is made available to those who wish to purchase goods.

It is sometimes suggested that any problem caused by insufficient demand can be solved by the actions of business firms themselves. All they have to do, it is claimed, is to increase continually the amount of money they invest. This solution actually denies the very aim of economic growth, which is to improve the situation of the citizen; but there is a more important reason why it is inappropriate—it would not work. Firms invest because they hope to be able to sell goods. If manufacturing machinery is bought in anticipation of an increase in consumer demand that is not realized, they will decide that further investment will be unprofitable and will therefore cut down their purchases. This will lead to decreases in buying in other areas of the economy and to a depression. The economy can therefore continue to develop only if investment and consumption demand grow together. The depression of the 1930's clearly demonstrates this fact; the oversupply of machinery was so great that there was practically no demand for new machines throughout the whole period.

In the postwar years the rise in available production has been largely taken up, partly because of the rise in population and tastes, partly because of the increase in government expenditures and the way in which these expenditures have been financed, and partly because of better understanding of the forces behind the business cycle. Will these factors continue to be equally important in future years or will they become less favorable? The last of these three forces will certainly increase in strength, for the willingness to plan for the long run rather than the immediate future is growing.

The future effect of increasing population and rising tastes is far more difficult to predict. The average family size continues to be larger than in the interwar period, despite the belief of many demographers that it was purely an immediate postwar phenomenon, and this has resulted in a rapid increase in population. However, prediction of future birth rates is essentially impossible, for they depend on the

views of each couple and society about the right size for the
family, and rapid changes can presumably take place. The
probable development of consumers' attitudes to additional
goods has also led to much controversy. Some commentators
claim that consumers are still interested in a higher standard
of living and that only the relative importance attached to
certain goods has changed. In his promotion of the "compact
car," George Romney, president of American Motors, stated,
"The automobile is no longer the means of satisfying the
ego of the American. The consumer is turning to swimming
pools and boats and trips to Europe and a lot of other things
besides automobiles." Romney claims that it was his understanding of this trend that enabled him to sell his smaller
compact car and that this also accounts for the eventual
decision of the big three to produce cars of this type.

It is certainly true that the American is turning to boats
and swimming pools. In five years the number of boats in
the United States has more than tripled, from 2,500,000 to
nearly 8,000,000, and the boom in sales is still growing. It
is estimated that in 1959 about two and a half billion dollars
was spent on boating. The number of swimming pools has
multiplied nine times between 1954 and 1958, and in 1959
alone the number of pools built was almost three times
greater than *existed* in 1954. Some observers believe, however, that these are just surface phenomena and the real
change is that the desire for goods in the United States is
decreasing. David Riesman wrote in the *Bulletin of the
Atomic Scientists:* "Contrary to the image envious non-
Americans often have, ferocious desire for things for their
own sake is declining, let alone desire for money or land
for its own sake. . . . Thus I suggest that there is a tendency
for people, once accustomed to upper-middle-class norms, to
lose zest for bounteous spending on consumer goods."

Others have suggested that, even if consumers' tastes are

still increasing rapidly, a change is overdue. Professor **Gal**-braith argues that much of the money now spent on consumption goods should be diverted to the purchase of items that are insufficiently provided for or supported by government expenditures: schools, colleges, slum clearance, control of pollution, town blight, etc. This proposed solution at least makes an attempt to deal with the problem that would arise if all individuals came to attach less importance to goods than in the past and saved more of the money they received. The resources on which they had claims but did not use would be taken over by the government and employed for social purposes. Such a suggestion, however. inevitably challenges conceptions of the limits of the role of government. Would it be wise or proper for it to move into fields from which it has previously been excluded or where its influence has been limited?

We have seen that the financing of government expenditures by progressive taxation caused a reduction in savings. Factors are still working to reinforce this trend, for the most wealthy people normally inherited their wealth and the existence of inheritance taxes will ensure that the fortune of the son will normally be smaller than that of the father. Income tax rates reach 91 per cent of income, and although their impact can be limited by capital gains provisions and other exemptions, any growth in income will normally increase the proportion paid in tax. The amount of saving carried out by the rich can therefore be expected to decline. Nevertheless, a recent survey in America showed a reversal of previous trends with an increase in the proportion of resources owned by the richest members of society, a development that follows from the fact that the effective rate of tax on large incomes is normally far less than one would expect from the theoretically extremely progressive tax structure. Changes in attitudes toward the right levels of wages and salaries have tended to limit income differentials between the manager and the worker in recent years and it may well be that this tendency will continue. These changes will lead to decreases in savings and decrease the possibility of depressions.

Other factors, however, may lead to increases in savings, and two of these are of major importance. The first is the increase in the number of people trying to provide security for themselves and their families by placing money in pension and insurance plans covering sickness, old age, and death. The sums put aside for these purposes are certain to increase as more people become convinced of the importance of security and can afford to put aside money. The second is the tendency of many firms to save a larger proportion of the sums they require for expansion from their profits rather than borrow them.

There have been so many violent changes in the underlying structure of the economies of the rich countries that the present practice of basing policies on crude parallels with the past has little relevance. The fact that inflation was caused by a shortage of goods in the nineteenth century does not mean that this is the reason for inflation in the twentieth. The basic conditions have changed.

Our economic shibboleths were derived from an economic system that assumed that the supply of goods and the demand for goods would automatically stay in balance. It is generally agreed that this condition is no longer fulfilled; governments must therefore accept responsibility for the maintenance of this balance between supply and demand. In these circumstances an unbalanced budget will not be synonymous with irresponsibility, nor will it always cause inflation. When the private demand for goods is insufficient to take up all the production that can be supplied by the available man-power and equipment, the government should use the spare capacity to meet desirable social goals.

The rate of growth of economies has been controlled for so long a period by the rate of growth in the potential supply of goods that it is difficult to adapt our economic thinking to the fact that the real determinant of growth in the rich countries is now the demand for the goods that can be produced. The industrial capacity exists in America at the present time to provide more consumer goods and more school buildings, more roads and more hospitals. Choices should normally be, not in terms of either-or, but in terms of what should be done with the growing abundance. During the latter half of the 1950's resources have lain idle in America because the economic system has not been adjusted so as to make more money available to those who wished to buy goods.

The scope for changes in the 1960's is made uncertain by the fact that alterations in the size of the arms budget cannot be adequately forecast. If tension declines—as is to be hoped —and with it expenditures on weapons, it is certain that the governments of all the rich countries would need to take drastic steps to avoid a slump. However, this does not mean that a reduction in tension *will* cause a slump—it means exactly what is said. The economies of the rich countries would not adjust automatically; governments would need to use some of the freed resources to meet desirable social goals—both national and international.

The major danger at the present time—a danger that is most acute in America but is present in the other rich countries—is that there is a tendency to assume that the closer the economy comes to the free competitive model of the nineteenth-century economist, the better the situation must be. Thus any decrease in the degree of government interference is assumed to be automatically good; it is not realized that it is in large measure the pattern of government interference that now keeps the economy operating.

A cut in armaments expenditure would open major new possibilities to every rich country. They would need to be evaluated in terms of their effect on the over-all economy. The major duty of the government would be to ensure that the effective demand within the economy continues to be sufficient to allow all those who wish to work to find a job, or, if they cannot, to ensure that they are provided with an adequate income.

The choices open to the government in obtaining this result will be varied; many of them will be novel and most of them will be in conflict with old slogans and beliefs. It would be possible to ensure, as Galbraith suggested, that the person who could not find a job because of generalized unemployment should receive almost as much money when out of work as when working. The government might attain its aim by increasing expenditures both in the fields where it has traditionally been active and in new areas where it feels that its help might be effective. The tax structure might be used to reduce inequality.

America will be able, for the first time, to provide freedom from want and fear of want for all its inhabitants. It will no longer be necessary to fail to grant a reasonable standard of living to the unemployed because of the fear that this might result in a lower rate of economic growth. Nor will it be necessary to refuse to supply medical care for all because this might interfere with the incentive to work. It will be possible to recognize that many are unfortunate through no fault of their own and that the aim of society must be to succor them and give them a possibility of regaining a useful place in the community. A major difficulty in the formulation of these new goals is that their acceptance will be impeded by the fact that they have frequently been labeled "communist" or "socialist." Unless we realize that these are merely epithets, they are likely to set us back in our search for a viable form of society in an affluent age.

Some of the implications of this affluence are discussed in the next chapter, but before leaving this one we must examine briefly the position in the rest of the rich countries. Is there the same possibility of insufficient demand, and if so, why has there been an almost continuous boom since the completion of the Marshall Plan? In Europe there has been a demand for all available goods; there has been no need to "sell." The amount of money put aside in savings has tended to be lower than the amount required for investment, there has been a shortage of investment funds in all the years since the war. This has been aggravated in many countries by considerable dissaving in the richer classes, who, knowing that much of their fortunes would pass into the hands of the state at their death preferred to spend them.

In addition, the other rich countries are behind the United States in their levels of material comfort. The inhabitants were made aware during and after the war of the higher standard of living achieved by America, and this lesson was reinforced by the passion for productivity and a rising income that swept Europe in the 1950's. The rich countries were determined to obtain a higher standard of living and have made great strides in this direction. However, the United States still leads, and while this is true it will be easier for the other rich countries to introduce new goods people will wish to buy.

Nevertheless, the possibility of production being greater than demand in these countries has not been banished. It has been kept under control by the fact that the maximum income that can be earned is lower than in the United States. However, by the end of the 1950's, supply largely caught up with demand in many of the rich countries, and the possibilities of depressions are therefore greater than at any time since before the war. Depressions could, however, be controlled as in the United States, by appropriate government action.

X. *Wealth and Leisure*

THROUGHOUT MAN'S HISTORY, most of his time was required to produce the food, clothing, and shelter he
needed to survive. In the past, small elites have sometimes
been supported in luxury by the remainder of the population, but only the rapid increase in production in the rich
countries has provided the prospect of freeing whole populations from the pressure of want. Already it is possible in
these countries for society to choose between leisure and the
manufacture of additional goods; the further increases in
production that can be forecast will still further augment
the possibility of choice.

The increase in wealth will allow action in areas where
it was previously impossible, but it also challenges us to
re-examine whether the maximum possible rate of growth
is now required. What is the purpose of economic development? Such a question often appears faintly ridiculous to

the inhabitants of the rich countries. The answer appears simple: economic growth makes it possible to provide more goods for each person, and the existence of these additional goods allows people to be happier than they would be without them. The question, however, is whether this relationship is valid for any level of production or whether the amount of additional satisfaction obtained from further increases in consumption falls off when a country already has a high standard of living?

It can be estimated that by the year 2,000, only forty years away—or just half the average lifetime of people in the rich countries—the standard of living can be expected to be anything from two to four times higher than it is at the present time, assuming that hours of work remain unchanged and the same importance continues to be attached to economic growth and wealth. This chapter explores the implications of this rate of growth and suggests the possibilities that will be opened to these societies because of them. One point at least is clear: this rapid increase in the national income will outdate the existing conventional wisdom, which is distilled from the experience of the past and will not apply in changed conditions.

What then are the outlines of the present situation in the rich countries? Ever since the Industrial Revolution productivity has been rising; apparently the rate of increase has been accelerating in recent years because of larger expenditures on scientific research and development work. Each year, therefore, a larger amount of goods and services can be produced with the same amount of work. This increase in potential production can be taken up in three ways. In some cases, workers may wish to take some of the advantage from the increase in productivity in the form of a shorter work week, work year, or work life. However, it is generally agreed that the decline in hours of work should be voluntary; each person has a right to an occupation if he wants one. The second possibility is for the community to consume a larger quantity of goods than it has done in the past. The third is that the rate of productivity increase should be deliberately slowed down so that the amount of goods or leisure that becomes available each year will be at a lower level than would otherwise have been the case. The reactions of most of those in the rich countries is that the third of these choices is ridiculous, and there are many suggestions that what is required is an increase and not a decrease in the rate of growth.

An examination of the implications of certain rates of growth may give us cause to reconsider. If a 5-per-cent increase in income were to be achieved in America in the next forty years—and this has been suggested by many commentators as a wise aim—each person would have to use up the equivalent of $9000 worth of goods per year if the average working week remained at forty hours; he would need to consume an average amount of $4500 if the working week were twenty hours. Even this latter figure is twice the present average. Assuming this rate of increase and a twenty-hour work week, the income of each individual would rise $200 every year—one tenth of his present total consumption. (These figures, resting on extrapolations of population, are not completely accurate; they aim to indicate only orders of magnitude.) The implications of increasing income can also be seen by examining probable changes in income during the next decade. *Fortune* magazine estimates that the amount of money available at the end of the 1960's for spending as the family wishes—"discretionary spending"—will be double that of the present day, suggesting that this may result in faddism, as people switch from one type of expenditure to another in order to keep in the swim.

These figures are at least sufficient to suggest that it is

necessary to compare the advantages of the maximum rise
in production—and its consequent increase in consumption
and leisure—with the gains obtainable from slower increases
in production. What proportion should we aim to achieve
among the various possibilities? The "conventional wisdom"
would, of course, demand that we take all steps to keep the
rate of increase of production as rapid as possible, thus
limiting the amount of hours we need to work and increasing the amount of goods we can consume at the greatest
attainable speed. But the conventional wisdom has never
been confronted with a situation in which man would have
little need to work and in which he can consume all the
goods he requires. It is at least legitimate to wonder whether
a life of this type would be found satisfactory by those living
in the rich countries and if it will be possible to introduce
such a drastic change of values within the lifetime of one
generation.

Part of the difficulty stems from the fact that we need
new concepts. Economic growth—and by extension social
welfare—has been calculated in the past by totaling the
value of all goods and services produced in the economy.
This was relatively satisfactory when the largest part of the
national income consisted of such items as food, clothing,
and other essentials of life. As we move further away from
this situation, the applicability of this concept as a measure
of growth is increasingly called in question. What is the
value of the services of an opera singer, a movie star, or a
surgeon? What is the worth of a university education, or
unspoiled countryside? To discuss the implications of further growth has become very difficult simply because money
is becoming an increasingly inadequate measure of the real
value of commodities and services.

It is often suggested that the socioeconomic problems of
the future should not take up time, that the year 2000 is a

long way off, and that the time could be better used for the examination of immediate problems. Society may not have been forced to think so far ahead in earlier centuries, for the child could expect that the values he learned in his youth would be valid throughout his life. However, if the year 2000 falls within an era of unparalleled abundance and leisure, the attitudes required will be radically different from those of the present day. We should not continue to teach children who will be the leaders in the year 2000, the ideas and ideals appropriate to an economy that is based on scarcity.

Before we can examine the correct course of action, we must discard the idea that economic growth is good in and of itself, that there is no need to justify it. Our present attitudes grew from the fact that it was never believed that man's efforts could provide a comfortable standard of living for each person. Economics was known throughout the nineteenth century as the "dismal science," for Malthus was thought to have proved that it was impossible for man ever to obtain more than a bare subsistence, that increases in population would inevitably be more rapid than the growth in production. As this belief has been shown to be false, it must also be recognized that economic growth can be useful only if it serves to promote the goals society wishes to attain.

The basic need for economic growth at the present time is often postulated on the need to protect and enhance the prestige of a country; this has most often been argued in the case of the United States. It is claimed that the American economy must stay as far ahead of the Russian economy as possible in order to protect itself from attack; as an alternative to or reinforcement of this point it is suggested that the rate of growth of the Western countries must be more rapid than the communist powers, for the poor countries will inevitably be attracted to the system that obtains the most rapid rate of growth. No individual, society, or country is wise to enter a competition it is bound to lose if it wants to preserve its morale. Russia will grow more rapidly than the West, not only because she devotes a greater proportion of her national income to investment but because she has a greater need for additional goods. Despite this fact America and other Western countries have often posed the conflict between them and Russia in terms of the amount of goods they will produce in the future.

The implications of this attitude are more serious than is generally realized. The Western countries have always proclaimed their aim to be an increase in the standard of living of the whole world; they have now maneuvered themselves into a position where they appear to disapprove of economic growth in the communist countries. Such an attitude can only damage the image that the West has fostered. It is also against their own best interests, for it has been historically true that those with most to lose from a war are least willing to accept strife, while those who are hungry and ill-clad will fight because they have nothing to lose.

Is rapid economic growth essential in order to influence the poor countries? It is argued by some that these countries will remain allied to the West only if they can see that the capitalist system is more efficient than the communist, but that if the communist system appears to produce the most rapid rate of growth they will use it. We have seen that the poor countries cannot adopt *either* the pure communist *or* the pure capitalist doctrines if they are to succeed in securing economic growth. Their specific problems will require solutions adapted to their particular situations, and to describe them as capitalist or communist can only confuse the issue.

More rapid growth in the rich countries might be proposed as a method of increasing the amount of aid that could be made available to the poor. But this would not improve the situation. The rich countries can already "afford" to give large sums of money to the poor; it is only the will and the institutions to do so that are missing. The introduction of new goods in the rich countries further increases the rate of growth of tastes in the poor and makes the task of satisfying them more difficult.

The poor countries cannot be expected to throw in their lot with either side in the cold war, for in the opinion of many of them the conflict is essentially false; both sides are responsible for promoting and continuing tension. The respect of the poor countries will be given to those nations that take the trouble to examine their real difficulties, who make genuine efforts to aid them in their nearly impossible task, and appreciate that many of the policies they follow are considered unpleasant and are accepted only because they constitute the least unsatisfactory available solution. Resentment will grow if nations try to dictate on ideological grounds the policies that should be followed, particularly when the acceptance of advice is a condition of giving aid.

The necessity for rapid growth cannot therefore be argued from its effectiveness as a weapon in the cold war; it must be based upon the needs of each country. While no nation has yet reached a situation where it can provide all the goods which are required by its inhabitants, the prospective growth in income during the next decades will bring many of them to a position where more rapid growth is not the major need; the most important problem will be to develop a social system in which the range of choice which is being opened by increasing wealth can be meaningfully used. Luis Marin, Governor of Puerto Rico, put it this way: "Let us enter this decade with the firm purpose of giving youth a good example of an attempt, a conscious and deliberate attempt, to begin subordinating the economy to the spirit."

One field in which action is urgently required is to help the poorer and less successful members of society. The rich countries have come to believe that they have a duty to help the unfortunate, but their actions have been restricted by the fear that, if aid were freely available from the community as a whole, the individual would be less concerned to help himself, and the society would therefore be deprived of the work that might have been contributed if money had not been given. It has been argued that strict limits should be placed on the amount of help society would make available and that a stigma should be attached to applying for aid. These arguments are no longer valid in an affluent society.

Governments will now be able to spend more to prevent the continuation of situations where poverty and want in one generation perpetuate misery and crime in the next. Impoverished communities cannot afford to provide the education that would make it possible for their children to rise above the problems of their parents; it is in this way that hatred and vice are continued from one generation to another. The distortion of the human spirit that comes from living in slums and being pressured into joining anti-social gangs—which are the only form of community life in many areas—far outweighs the costs of providing the necessary schools and tearing down substandard housing and replacing it. Private and social benefits often diverge at the present time; government intervention is therefore necessary and will become more vital as this divergence grows wider. Reliance on free competition is outdated; the necessary conditions no longer exist to make it possible to prove that it would maximize the satisfaction of the community. In particular, the idea that a self-regulating mechanism exists that distributes world wealth fairly among countries is invalid. Free competition will not maximize the welfare of the world, and poor countries will need help from the rich if they are to develop.

In the long run, the problem of the rich countries will be to examine and challenge the ideology that makes work more important than leisure and suggests that consumption is valuable of itself without reference to the services that can be rendered by the goods purchased. It will be necessary to see what aims the individual should adopt to make sense of his life, whether there are ways in which he can spend his days happily without working or whether a certain amount of labor would add to his satisfaction. This does not mean than an attempt should be made to destroy the idea of the dignity of work, the sense of achievement that comes from a job well done; indeed, there is perhaps a need to rebuild this ideal, which has been tarnished by the prevalence of mass-production techniques, where the individual attends a factory only in order to be able to obtain the consumption goods he wants rather than to gain any satisfaction from work. Some would argue that this is not the moment to raise such questions, that it is too soon to tell whether new consumption needs will be developed to take up all the available production, and too early to challenge the ethic that has made work, saving, and consumption into a way of life. This view is unrealistic; events are forcing this reconsideration—the younger generation is no longer satisfied with the old aims, believing that they are inadequate. Even if this were untrue, we could not afford to delay our re-examination, for ideas do not change instantaneously.

In the past most individuals were able to go through life with the set of attitudes and beliefs appropriate to the age in which they were brought up. The rate of change in science, in technology, in the beliefs and ideals of man was sufficiently slow to ensure that they remained relatively appropriate. Even then the older generation expressed its dissatisfaction in the phrase: "I don't know what the world is coming to." Nowadays it is recognized that the attitudes appropriate to the beginning of the twenty-first century will be totally different from those now accepted, but little attempt is made to look ahead. Indeed, much education is based on the ideas of past scholars; as a result theories are taught to generations of students long after they have been recognized by the leaders in the field of study to be incorrect.

Work and consumption will continue to be accepted for many years in the rich countries; indeed it appears that more importance has been given to them in Europe in the years since the war than in the past. Never has so much attention been paid to the need for additional production and higher productivity in order to attain the American standard of living. In the House of Commons in England in the 1950's, the Prime Minister could sum up the economic goals of his government in the statement that it was hoped to double the standard of living in the next twenty-five years—an inconceivable attitude before the war but one that reflects the greatly increased interest in material well-being.

The major problem of the rich and poor countries is basically the same, the need to develop new values more suitable for the age in which we live. The problems we now face in the rich countries will become important in the poor as their economic development continues. In the past, the social balance was maintained through the acceptance of traditional values passed down within the closely knit rural community or primitive tribe. However, the explosive rate of change and rapid economic development have already challenged many of these values, and there is a need for their replacement by others that must act, as did the old, to permit individual self-expression in forms that will not be detrimental to society as a whole.

The destruction of accepted standards of behavior has been more complete in the rich countries, and our failure to find new ones to take their place has led to the apparent paradox of the individual in the rich countries, who, theoretically unrestricted in his choice of behavior and actions, is actually more conformist and less individualistic than a tradition-oriented member of a primitive tribe. Knowledge of tribal tradition provides the individual with the sense of security necessary to mental well-being and allows the expression of individualism. In Western society the necessity for this mental and moral support from one's fellow-men is often expressed in the individual's desire for acceptance within social groups. It is often difficult, however, to discern which of the group's behavior patterns are central and which peripheral, with the result that an individual models the totality of his behavior on the observable standards of the group, suppressing the expression of individualistic traits.

Individual self-expression is possible only when people know what is expected of them and are aware of the goals to which they should aspire. As the old accepted beliefs and aims of the rich countries have been destroyed or made inappropriate by the process of economic growth and the development of scientific knowledge, we must discover others more relevant to the age in which we live. What methods can be used? Only a new type of education that, instead of teaching facts or methods—how to do things—will instead develop values—or why actions should be taken. The way of life of each generation is now separated from that of the previous one by so wide a gulf that the beliefs accepted by parents will not be adequate for their children.

The generation that is now being educated will live into an age when money will cease to be an adequate measure of the value of goods—if indeed it ever was; when greater production and productivity will cease to be a major goal;

when hours of work will be less than half those of the present time and the success of society will depend on its ability to enjoy leisure; when space travel will be a possibility. Their education must fit them to deal with the complexities of this future world.

This generation will have to face even greater problems; they must decide what use they will make of the new scientific knowledge that is now being developed. During the next forty years it may become possible to alter a human being so that he becomes more intelligent, stronger, or has some other "desirable" combination of characteristics. Should limits be imposed to this kind of action? If science can find a way to improve our children, should we take it? Is this picture drawn in *Brave New World* a nightmare only because we have not lived in it? At any rate the problem is posed. Philip Siekevits, a biologist at the Rokefeller Institute, expressed it in these words: ". . . man is about to change his biological environment as radically as he is now changing his physical environment . . . we will be able to plan ahead so that our children will be what we would like them to be—physically and even mentally . . ."

"Man does not live by bread alone . . ." These are words that in the past sometimes seemed to be a mockery of man's efforts—too few have had sufficient bread. We can already see in the future, assuming that there is no war, an age where man will have all the food he requires. But he will still be unable to live on materialism alone; it will be vital to have a clear goal. In the immediate future the challenge of building a world in which all can have sufficient food, clothing, and shelter will appear to need all our attention. Unless we think ahead to the time when these problems are already solved, we will not know how to make sense of man's life. The richest countries of the world are not the most satisfied.

Part III

INTERNATIONAL RELATIONS

XI. *The Inapplicability of the Dogma of Free Trade*

W E HAVE SEEN how the existing social attitudes of the poor countries are unlikely to lead to the rapid rate of growth required to meet the needs of the rising population and to satisfy their increasing desire for better health, more education, and Western-type consumption goods. We have seen that the rich countries, which have attained a reasonable standard of living, will be able to pay less attention to attaining the highest possible rate of growth and more to the fairer distribution of the benefits from the high standard of living—eliminating poverty, depressed areas, and slums. In a world in which the problems and potentialities of various groups of countries are so different a pressing question must be answered: How should the economic relationships between them be arranged? The conventional response is that free competition must be allowed to determine the prices of goods produced in the various countries of the world, that any attempt to interfere with the prices so determined will decrease the welfare of the population of the world as a whole, and that there must be no interference with trade—"free trade" must prevail. But this theory is valid only when neoclassical assumptions are realistic, and this is no longer the case.

In reappraising the proper relations between countries it is necessary to return and examine the way in which the theory of free trade developed. It was based on the nineteenth-century situation where differences in the prices of goods depended very largely on the availability of better grades of raw materials or the more suitable natural conditions in one country for producing certain crops. The original case for free trade did not consider the result of industrialization, that as it progressed the inhabitants of certain countries would become skilled, through *experience,* in the production of various types of goods. If another country took up the manufacture of any of these goods at a later date, the cost of production would normally be higher in the initial stages because of the lack of training of factory workers and management.

Recognition of this relationship led economists to introduce the first exception into the basic theory of free trade; it was christened the "infant-industry argument." It came to be agreed that if an industry were to be eventually profitable in any country, it would be justifiable to protect it from foreign competition when it was first set up—either by an outright ban on imports or by a tax. This would allow the new industry time to become efficient. However, a difficult issue was raised by this exception. How long does an infant industry remain young and entitled to protection? This question eventually proved insoluble because of an inherent flaw in the original conception. The infant industry argument has logical extensions that result in its development into an "infant-country argument."

Economic growth sets up two contrary sets of forces; one tending to increase the cost of production, the other to reduce it. The increase in costs comes from the rising wages that accompany economic growth. The tendency toward a reduction results from increasing efficiency, which is caused by the spread of education and the creation of new skills, by an increase in the amount of equipment available to each worker, and by bringing into existence specialized auxiliary firms whose services are available to all at prices far lower than the individual enterprise would have to pay if it employed its own specialists in the various subjects.

How does this come about? Adam Smith provided the explanation almost two hundred years ago; a rise in the demand for a product makes it possible for several individuals to collaborate in its production; each individual will become more skilled and productive as the range of actions he does is reduced. Adam Smith expressed this in an axiom: "The division of labor depends upon the extent of the market." His argument was primarily in terms of the individual, for this was the relevant unit at the time he wrote; nowadays it is more usually the firm. Specialized services become economical as the size of the market increases; firms can be set up to design crates or boxes, to prepare an advertising campaign, to study the size of the market for new products or the efficiency of a mill; others will be able to concentrate on the production of identical or similar parts used in the manufacture of different products. There will be more reliable transport and power services and the area in which they are available will grow. The increasing intensity of education and training will make more skilled people available to each firm and provide technicians and scientists who can be employed to solve production problems and to design and invent new products.

There can be no certainty that an enterprise will be able to gain higher profits by setting up a factory in a poor country than in a rich one; the advantages to be gained from lower wages may be offset by a lack of managerial and technical knowledge and by the absence of ancillary skills and necessary services. Even where profits would be higher in the poor countries, there may be certain other factors that decrease or nullify this advantage—the difficulty of importing goods required for operations because of quota or licensing regulations, the possibility that the transfer abroad of profits might be hampered, and in certain cases the fear of interference in methods of operation and even nationalization of the factory. There will, however, be some cases where the difference in profits will be very substantial; this will most often be true for raw materials that are not available in competitive grades in the rich countries.

Professor Myrdal, accepting essentially the "infant-country argument," challenged the traditional neoclassical economic concept that argues that free competition would suffice to pull the more poverty-stricken countries up to the higher levels reached elsewhere in the world. He stated that it had been generally believed that lower wages in the poor countries will allow them to produce goods at cheaper prices than was possible in the rich countries. He suggests that this is not true; the lack of skills and services ensures that the cost of production will be above that of the rich countries in many cases; only by providing sufficient education and training can the poverty and misery of the poor countries be conquered. He equates the problems of the poor countries with those that occur in a poor area within a rich country, arguing that the cure will not come from leaving the situation alone but by intervention to break up the vicious circle that tends to perpetuate the situation.

It would therefore appear that the assumptions required to prove that free competition and free trade will act to maximize the welfare of the world are not fulfilled; how then can we discover the pattern that would be most effective in ensuring this result? We must return to first principles and re-examine the advantages and disadvantages of securing goods from abroad. The first advantage is the ability to purchase goods that cannot be produced in the home country. America either lacks totally or has insignificant deposits of nineteen out of the thirty-two most vital minerals used in her industries. Similar figures obtain in many other rich countries. In the poor countries there are no facilities at the present time for producing certain vital machinery. If international trade did not provide a method of exchanging these goods, manufacture of many products would become infinitely more expensive and in some cases impossible; the result would be an immediate and heavy fall in the standard of living.

This, however, is not the only advantage obtained by purchasing goods abroad. International trade permits international specialization of labor; those countries with the best grades of various raw materials will sell them abroad, those with the most suitable climate for the production of certain agricultural crops can concentrate on their production. The purchase of lower-priced goods from abroad will make it possible to raise the standard of living throughout the world. The production of the imported goods would have been expensive in terms of labor and resources; the possibility of importing goods from abroad will allow available resources to be concentrated in industries where they would be most efficient. For example, it would be extremely costly for America to create artificially the conditions needed for the production of tea. Because of international trade all nations will be able to purchase and use more goods than would have been possible if international trade had not existed—all countries gain from the exchange.

This second benefit will exist *only* if a country is able to re-employ the people freed from their old work by the imports of lower-priced goods. If they are thrown out of work and are unable to find another occupation, international trade will have worsened the country's situation. An analogy will illustrate this argument. A person in a well-paid job will be willing to employ specialized workers to do certain jobs in his house; it will be cheaper for him in time and money to hire somebody to labor for him than take time to do it himself. If, however, he is out of work and unable to obtain employment, he will be wise to do the necessary jobs himself even though he may be relatively inefficient. In the same way, countries with unemployment or underemployment may not gain any advantage by allowing cheaper goods to be imported to take the place of goods they could produce themselves at higher prices by using the labor that would otherwise be unemployed and contribute nothing to the economy.

While many economists still argue that free trade is the best policy, they do not deny the possibility that the supply of foreign exchange and the demand for it may get out of balance. With present international trade rules this means that the country concerned will be unable to buy the goods it urgently needs. It will be possible to see more clearly whether free trade is practicable at the present time if we examine the methods economists claim could be used to balance the supply of and demand for foreign exchange. One suggestion is that the demand for goods within a country should be reduced; the demand for imports would thus be cut down and the amount of goods available for export increased. However, the first economic imperative in the poor countries, which suffer from an acute shortage of foreign exchange, is to maintain and increase their level of production, for this is the only way they will be able to satisfy their growing needs. This method of making free trade work would therefore be inappropriate in most cases. It would also usually be ineffective. There may, however, be occasions when rich countries, suffering from a shortage of foreign exchange, should follow a policy of reducing demand.

The second policy usually proposed is that the value of the currency should be decreased (devalued) so that the amount of a foreign currency that can be purchased with one unit of the home currency declines. (In a devaluation of the pound sterling, for example, the inhabitants of all other countries would give a smaller amount of their currency to purchase one pound after the devaluation than before it.) It is argued by economists that the position of the devaluing country will be improved by this step: other countries will be willing to buy more of the goods produced in the devaluing country for they will now appear cheaper, while the inhabitants of the devaluing nation will not want to purchase as many goods from abroad, for they will appear more expensive compared to those produced at home.

In reality this policy usually aggravates the over-all problem of the country with a shortage of foreign exchange. It is like saying to a peasant family that is unable to purchase all the goods it requires that the cure for its condition is to decrease the price for which it sells its produce while offering to pay more for the articles it needs. The position of the family *cannot* be improved by such a step although it could help to bring the expenditure and receipts of the family into balance in certain circumstances. The end result *might* be that the family would balance its receipts and its expenditures but only at the cost of extra work and a lower standard of living. Judgment of the suggestion would then depend on whether it would be wise for the position of this family to be made worse relative to other families; if this were felt to be unjust, it would be better to impose direct restrictions on the amount of goods each member of the family was allowed to purchase. This, in effect, is what almost all families do; for the amount of goods they would like to buy exceeds the amount of money available to purchase them.

We must not allow the greater complexity of the economy of a country compared to a family to blind us to the fact that its situation is similar. Just as the family would like to buy more goods than it can afford, so in many cases would the inhabitants of the poor countries like to import more goods from abroad. The country faces the same two alternatives as the family, it can either pay more for what it buys and obtain less for what it sells (devalue the currency) or it can limit the amount of purchases people are allowed to make. The decision of a country, however, will be complicated by the fact that a certain number of people will always consider it worthwhile to smuggle goods—thus lessening the effect of the restriction.

The decrease in the price of goods produced by a peasant family and the increase in the price paid for the goods purchased by it can bring the income and the expenditure of the family into balance only if it is able to increase the amount it sells and decrease the amount it buys. In the same way the balance-of-payments position of a country cannot be improved by devaluation if the country does not find that its imports are decreased and exports increased. However, in many of the countries that suffer from a shortage of foreign exchange—particularly the poor ones—all the available productive equipment is already being used; exports are limited by non-availability rather than price. Neither can the production within the country of goods previously imported from abroad be encouraged by this step, because the necessary raw materials may not be available and the factories to produce the required articles not yet built. If any country that is already using all its productive capacity consents to a reduction in the price it requires for its exports and an increase in the price it is willing to pay for its imports, it will decrease the amount of goods it can make available to the population without bringing the demand for foreign exchange into balance with its supply.

The factors causing trade deficits can be illustrated by the course of American-European trade since the war. At its end all the countries of Europe suffered from an acute shortage of goods and were willing to import products from any country that would provide the goods regardless of the price demanded. The only country where surplus goods were available for export was the United States, and there was therefore a long period during which the demand for American goods was far greater than could be paid for by sales to the United States. The resulting pressure on the dollar reserves of many European countries led to a devaluation of their currencies in 1949. Despite this step the dollar gap persisted; many economists came to believe that it was a permanent phenomenon. In recent years, however, production in European countries has greatly increased and it is no longer necessary to import goods to meet acute scarcities. For example, emergency imports of American coal, which were very large until late in the 1950's, had become totally unnecessary by the end of this decade because of the excessive stocks in all the European countries. On the other hand, exports from Europe to America increased rapidly in the last part of the 1950's and show every promise of rising still further, for wages in Europe are so low compared to United States levels that many goods can be produced more cheaply in these countries than in America. One of the most remarkable changes has been in the field of automobile sales. In 1953 the United States exported five times as many cars as it imported, but by 1958 imports were four times exports. As a result of these changes, the problem of the dollar gap in relation to Europe has steadily faded and the economic discussions of the early 1960's will concentrate on ways of preventing the flow of goods from Europe to America from becoming so large as to threaten trade equilibrium. It may eventually prove necessary to reverse the devaluation that took place in European countries; alternatively it may prove wise for America to devalue the dollar.

We can see from the above analysis that two different sets of circumstances can result in trade deficits. The problem in Europe in the years after the war was caused by a shortage of goods—price was relatively unimportant; while the recent American balance-of-payments problem reflects the classical economic analysis—prices are out of line in Europe and America. When the difficulties are caused by prices being out of line, a change in the relative values of the currencies of the two countries will help to bring imports and exports back into balance; when the problem is a shortage of goods, devaluation will not be suitable, for it will worsen the position of the devaluing country.

In the poor countries there will be a permanent tendency for the demand for goods to be greater than the available supply. The existence of a balance-of-payments deficit will not be conclusive evidence of the need for devaluation in a poor country, for the balance of payments will often be continuously in deficit. In addition, measures to bring supply and demand into balance will normally be inappropriate, for this will be possible only by restricting or inhibiting the rate of growth. The only acceptable way to balance imports and exports will be by protection.

Confronted with this argument, some economists would say that they have always recognized that the position of any country could be improved by imposing protection but that the condition of the rest of the world would be worsened by this step; in addition they might argue that the position of the country that first protected its commerce would probably also be damaged in the long run because other countries would retaliate. It is, however, possible to improve the situation of the world as a whole by protection, for the free-trade theory is based on the belief that there could be no unemployment or underemployment in any country. If this is not true, protection will make it possible for additional people to be brought into the labor force and an increase in world production to occur. The poor countries will need to follow protectionist policies as long as they remain poor. On the other hand, the rich countries benefit from free trade, for they can maintain full employment by appropriate government action; those workers released by imports can be employed elsewhere in the economy. The combination of free trade in the rich countries and protection for the poor will benefit *both* sets of countries; neither will suffer.

The acceptance of protection as the right policy for the poor countries involves the danger that inefficient industries will be left undisturbed, and that they will be allowed to sell their goods at a price that is well above that dictated by foreign competition. This problem can be alleviated by creating common markets between countries at roughly comparable levels of development; in this way some of the benefits of specialization can be secured. It will be important for all the countries within the common market to have roughly the same ratio of available capital to labor, for unless this is so there will be economic tension among the various countries and escape clauses will be continuously invoked. If the common market is successful, it will be possible for an industry to be set up in one country to supply all the members; this cannot be done at the present time, for import quotas are so small and tariffs so high that imports are kept to a minimum. The usefulness of common markets is being considered and there is some chance of success in such areas as Central and South America, Africa, the Middle East, and parts of Asia as well as in Europe.

In certain poor countries, particularly those that are rich in oil resources, the availability of foreign exchange causes no difficulties; however, its very abundance raises its own problems, allowing more rapid action but requiring greater wisdom from those leading the country. In other countries, such as Jamaica with its bauxite and Ghana with its cocoa, the foreign-exchange resources are more limited but sufficient to allow growth. Elsewhere the problem of securing sufficient foreign exchange will be acute because of the non-existence of any raw materials in commercial quantity or quality and few if any export crops. Three examples of countries in this situation are Yugoslavia, Israel, and Pakistan; progress in such countries will depend to a large extent on programs of industrialization, which have proved difficult to implement, or on large amounts of foreign aid.

Japan's problems are unique at the present time. Her inability to obtain the rate of growth that would otherwise be possible stems directly from the unwillingness of other countries to buy Japanese goods despite their low costs, and from the imposition of direct controls by other countries on Japanese imports. The Japanese are willing to save—their saving rate has been one of the highest in the world since the war despite their comparative poverty—and they are willing to work hard. The main factor limiting their rate of economic growth is lack of foreign exchange to purchase the raw materials and machinery needed to open and operate new factories.

The restrictions on imports from Japan have sometimes taken the form of quantitative restrictions imposed by government order; in other cases a statement has been discretely conveyed that, if Japanese exports were to exceed a certain level, the foreign government would find it difficult to prevent pressure from the industry concerned from forcing them to limit Japanese imports. In America, for example, the agreement for the limitation of textile imports from Japan was termed "voluntary"; the government claimed that it was not involved, although the negotiations were held under the wing of the Department of Commerce. The desire to be in a position to discriminate against Japanese low-priced goods is so great that several countries refused to enter into treaty relations with Japan in the General Agreement on Trade and Tariffs, for this would have obligated them to accord her as favorable treatment as that given to all other countries.

Why are the rich countries unwilling to accept Japanese goods, which would make it possible to provide the public with articles it wants to buy at a lower price, thus raising the standard of living? The question may be widened by asking why *any* increase in imports is usually opposed. Industry hastens to protect its own market when it is threatened by imports, knowing that, although the public will be better off, the profits of their firm will be limited and they might even be forced out of business. It is natural, therefore, to take all possible steps to limit any increase in purchases from abroad. As long as firms and their workers suffer if increased imports are allowed, they must be expected to resist; it is only when government accepts some responsibility in this field that co-operation can reasonably be expected.

A change from producing certain types of goods at home

to importing them from abroad will never be costless in terms of economic welfare. The fact that textiles are now imported into the rich countries in larger quantities than in previous years has wrought great hardship on mills in Britain and America. Economists have often ignored this aspect of the situation when discussing the benefits of free trade. Although foreign trade *will* increase the welfare of the country as long as unemployment can be avoided, there is a strong case for governmental compensation of those who suffer when larger imports are allowed. It is now accepted that if a road is cut through private property the individual has a right to receive payment for the inconvenience caused; government changes in tariff and quota rates are equally destructive to the firm.

The recognition of the fact that the poor countries will normally need to import more goods than they can afford to buy raises new problems that economics has hardly begun to consider. Perhaps the most urgent will be to find ways of determining which goods should be imported; there will always be a shortage of foreign exchange, and therefore it will be necessary to ration the amount of goods that may be brought into the country. Merchants who are granted import licenses to obtain goods abroad are often able to sell the imported articles at prices far above those they paid for them and will therefore gain an excessive profit. This appears to be neither fair nor wise; it lays an additional strain on the civil servants of the country, for they must decide which individuals should benefit from this extra profit—to say nothing of the challenge to their honesty, since each merchant will be in a position to offer large bribes in order to obtain the valuable licenses.

It would seem logical that the profit from a shortage of foreign exchange should not accrue to a small group, but to the nation as a whole. This result can be achieved by

levying fixed taxes on different types of goods; alternatively
—and this is perhaps a better solution—by regularly auction-
ing off the scarce supplies of the foreign currency necessary
to buy goods abroad to the highest bidder. The person willing to pay the highest price in national currency would
obtain supplies of foreign currency. In this way the state
would gain additional revenue and the profits of the merchants be limited.

Nevertheless, allocations of foreign exchange will have
to be made for certain products. Individuals wishing to import essential food supplies or machinery should not be
forced to compete for foreign exchange with importers of
automobiles and other luxury goods who will be able to
obtain inflated prices. The step that is immediately necessary
is to admit the principle that scarce foreign exchange ought
in some circumstances to be rationed by price—a conclusion
that is denied by most economists despite their reliance on
the price mechanism in all other fields. Analysis of the
proper patterns of restriction will become far easier once
this arbitrary shibboleth has been removed.

At present the major problem in gaining the maximum
benefit from available foreign currency is that governmental
and intergovernmental authorities as well as many economists often argue that the use of protective methods is wrong
and that they should be abolished in the near future. The
whole weight of economic orthodoxy lies on the side of free
trade, and those economists who suggest new methods of
maximizing the welfare of a population under a protective
policy fail to find acceptance for their views. The basic
economic fact in the poor countries is that of scarcity; they
simply do not produce enough at the present time to gain
enough foreign exchange to enable them to import all the
goods they want and need for their industrialization and
to raise the standard of living. Nor is there any prospect

of a sufficiently rapid growth in national production in most
poor countries to alter this situation for many years. Protection will therefore be required, but it must be imposed
in such a way as to minimize the inevitable unfavorable
economic results, particularly those caused by the limitations
on foreign competition.

The connection between economic growth, protection,
and inflation can be shown by Brazil's experience. Brazil
claims to have boosted its national income 63 per cent in
the last ten years and income per head some 30 per cent.
Automobile production went from zero in 1955 to 66,316
in 1958, and it is hoped that it will reach 274,000 in 1961.
The appliance industry, which hardly existed in 1955,
turned out 21,000 vacuum cleaners, 50,000 washing machines, 135,000 floor waxers, 150,000 television sets, 200,000
refrigerators, 300,000 electric mixers, 631,000 sewing machines, and 660,000 radios in 1958. Meanwhile the cost of
living has moved up 365 per cent over 1948, while the
foreign trade balance has changed from a $248-million ex-
cess of exports over imports to an excess of imports over
exports of $166 million in 1958.

Even this evolution has been possible *only* because the
United States has been willing to give generous support to
Brazil—aid reaching $600 million in 1958—and Brazil's
raw-material-rich territory encouraged foreigners to invest
one and three-quarter billion dollars there in the last four
years. Without this aid, growth would have been slowed
down by a shortage of foreign exchange, as it has been in
many other parts of the world, for example in India and
Pakistan.

Many of the suggestions made in this chapter will certainly be opposed by the neoclassical economist, for it is
accepted that growth in the poor countries will normally
be accompanied by inflation and disequilibrium in the

balance of payments. The neoclassical economist would argue that these results should be avoided. However, we have seen that the poor countries need rapid economic growth if they are to survive politically and economically. An adequate rate of growth will be possible only by forcing the pace; this will normally lead to an excess of demand over supply within the country and to inflationary pressure and balance-of-payments difficulties. The neoclassical position amounts therefore to the statement that the rate of growth should be decreased in order to preserve stable prices and a balance in the field of foreign exchange. The choice is therefore not *economic* but *political.*

With the exception of a very few raw-material-rich countries, the foreign exchange that the poor countries can earn will not be adequate to allow them to import the goods they require if they are to attain the rate of growth they feel is necessary for the security of their country and the welfare of their inhabitants. Only if the rich countries supplement the resources available for development will growth under democratic patterns of government be possible: if these countries do not receive such funds, they will fall back into anarchy or growth will be obtained by dictatorial means.

The rich countries can provide resources and buy time for the poor. The need for help cannot be determined, as it has often been in the past, by whether the country has followed a policy that avoided both inflation and balance-of-payments difficulties, for such a criterion often deprives countries of aid at a moment when their economies are most severely in disequilibrium.

Growth in the poor countries cannot normally be achieved without protection and will almost always result in inflation; the degree of protection and of inflation will largely depend on the amount of aid granted.

XII. *The Benefits of International Giving*

THE POOR COUNTRIES will normally be unable to obtain the minimum rate of growth necessary to avoid social breakdown without help from the rich countries. Why should rich countries grant this aid? There are many who deny that they are either obligated or indeed wise to contribute funds to poor countries. Sometimes their argument rests on a general statement that the plight of the poor countries is their own concern and that there should be, as George Kennan phrased it, no sense of "cosmic guilt or obligation vis-a-vis the underdeveloped countries of the world." In other cases the argument is based on practical grounds; it is suggested that it is not useful to give or lend to the poor countries, as they will waste what they receive. Instances of inefficiency are cited to document this argument. That waste and inefficiency do exist is certainly true, but to destroy programs of international aid on these grounds would be unreasonable. The Draper Committee, set up in 1958 to report to President Eisenhower on this subject, agreed that, although inefficiency sometimes occurred, this was no reason to drop the programs, but only to make certain that they were better managed in the future.

Arguing that funds should not be withdrawn because of the existence of waste and inefficiency will not prove that the rich countries *should* give money to the poor. The best case for extension of international aid rests on our moral obligations. At the present time the conscience of society is still largely conterminous with national borders. While it is generally accepted that the inhabitants of each country have a duty to make sure that their fellow-citizens do not starve, there has been little development of values that consider suffering in all countries of the world equally distressing. If, however, a duty toward one's fellow-countrymen is accepted, surely a loyalty toward all human beings follows logically—extension will be only a matter of time and increasing knowledge. If it is denied that there is any need to help the unfortunate, it makes sense to argue that there is no necessity to help the poor countries; when there is a recognition that no fellow-citizen should starve, it is surely illogical to believe that help should be limited to those within national boundaries.

It is sometimes suggested that the poor countries are responsible for their own situation, because if they would only work and save they could provide for themselves. This is unrealistic; the two most important factors that have made economic growth essential in the poor countries are the increase in tastes and the reduction of the death rate without a corresponding limitation of the birth rate; both these changes were basically caused by contact with the West. It is the consequent explosive growth in population and tastes that has destroyed the virtue of the old value-systems and forced these countries to strive for rapid economic growth. Their values, which emphasize realities other than the need for a higher standard of living, cannot be expected to change within a short period of time; only the rich countries have sufficient funds to allow them to attain the necessary rate of growth while limiting the unfavorable effects on the social structure.

If these arguments do not appear adequate, aid can be shown to accord with the selfish interests of the rich countries. The inhabitants of the poor countries are no longer content to be regarded as second-class world citizens, and they include a higher material standard of living in their conception of a better way of life. If their wants are not satisfied, the world cannot expect peace; if despair is deep enough, war and revolution appear both logical and inevitable. The poor countries must be helped; this should be done because it is morally right; however, for those who do not recognize such claims, arguments from pure self-interest exist.

There are, however, several ways in which the position of the poor countries can be improved without harming the position of the rich. The first step would be for the rich countries to increase the amount of imports they are willing to accept from the poor. The old doctrine that trade advantages given to any country should be extended to all others must be abandoned: the rich countries of the world must be allowed to discriminate in favor of the poor and against the rich. There is no danger that the poor countries will build up surplus resources as a result of such changes; all the money available will be spent on increasing imports.

Imports into the rich countries should not be allowed to rise at such a rate as to cause general unemployment; this result can normally be avoided in the rich countries by appropriate government action. In addition, we saw that a policy of increasing imports would need to be planned in such a way that the damage to the firm and the worker was minimized. Government compensation would sometimes be required in areas where certain industries are heavily concentrated; special retraining programs might also be necessary.

The relaxation of import restrictions in the rich countries is often opposed on the grounds that it might leave a country without certain vital productive equipment if a war should break out. Apart from the fact that this argument is often invoked when the materials concerned would be of little importance, it fails to take into account the full extent of change since the last world conflict. If the war were of a limited nature, the sea lanes would remain open and imports would continue to be possible; in the case of a hydrogen bomb attack by the great powers it is wishful thinking to suggest that the amount of available production facilities would have anything to do with the result of the war.

A second step that could help the poor countries would be to develop equipment suitable for the scarcity of capital and superabundance of labor in these countries. At present almost all the machinery available for purchase is designed for highly skilled workers in countries with a comparative abundance of capital and a highly organized transport system. It would seem that it might be useful to set up an international Industrial Research Division, within the United Nations or one of the other international bodies, which would commission manufacturers to design machinery appropriate for the very different conditions in the poor countries at the present time.

A third step that would improve the situation of the poor countries would be to set up plans that would stabilize the price of the various metals and crops that are traded at the present time on world markets, to prevent violent fluctuations from year to year. Such a program would allow the poor countries to have an approximate idea of the amount they would receive for each of their products for some period ahead; this would contrast with the present situation, where the return from sales of export products may be halved within a single year. It has been estimated that the loss in receipts resulting from lower prices of raw materials during the 1958 recession was greater than the total amount received by the poor countries in foreign aid in that year.

It is often argued that it is impossible to set up plans of price stabilization because fluctuations in supply and demand are so great that a disastrous shortage or surplus of the products would sooner or later occur. There are two reasons why these plans are more possible now than they have ever been in the past. There is a world-wide determination to avoid a catastrophic slump and even major fluctuations in business activity. These two causes have—together with wars—accounted for the most violent movements in the price of materials in the past. In addition, the rich countries can now afford to stockpile raw materials for a time. Exact efficiency, which would consist in mining or producing exactly the right amount, can give way to ensuring that each of the poor countries would have some idea of the prices it would receive for its exports in coming years.

One of the few unilateral steps the poor countries can take to improve their position without outside help is to re-examine their attitude to allowing foreigners to invest capital in their countries. Investment in the poor countries is often not very attractive when firms are considering establishing subsidiaries. In many cases, profits from operating in the poor countries are smaller or not much greater than those available in the rich. Even if possible profits do seem greater, non-economic factors (such as the fear of penal taxation or nationalization) tend to stop the entrepreneur from situating his factory in a poor country. One of the most satisfactory methods poor countries can use to secure a higher rate of growth is to attract private investment, offering terms that specify the maximum tax liabilities over a period of years, and also give a guarantee of freedom from nationalization. Where this is impossible the terms on which nationalization could take place (if this were deemed essential in the national interest) should be stated. Such ideas have been adopted with notable success by many countries.

In return, the poor countries could request that foreign firms train a certain number of local technicians and administrators. It may, however, be unwise to insist, as is often done at present, that the direction of the foreign firm should be entirely taken over by the nationals of the poor countries after a number of years. For the shortage in the poor countries is of trained personnel; there will be many vital posts in the economy that cannot be filled. A more logical system might often be to insist that trained personnel should *not* be held in one factory but be allowed to take jobs in others or to set up their own firms.

The policy actually followed by the poor countries is often based on the idea that, if a foreign enterprise takes over one type of activity, there will be fewer jobs for their citizens. In actual fact the result of progress in one field is to make production of other types of goods profitable. The only occasion when a government might be wise to refuse permission for foreigners to operate in its country would be when a firm wished to mine or exploit raw materials, and where it would be possible for a national to carry out this work within a reasonable period of time.

The setting up of certain industries might also be discouraged, regardless of whether the person concerned were a citizen or a foreigner, if it might increase the strain on the balance of payments.

All the methods discussed so far have the considerable advantage of increasing the income of the poor countries without direct action by governments; diplomatic discussions about the amount to be transferred by foreign aid would not be necessary. The poor countries feel that the returns from international trade and investment come to them as a right, while the funds they obtain from aid are often considered humiliating. Nevertheless foreign aid will also be necessary and in increasing amounts, although the total sums that can be absorbed by the poor countries in the immediate future are limited. In a study commissioned by the United States Senate from the Center for International Studies of the Massachusetts Institute of Technology, it was suggested, "The capacity of underdeveloped countries to absorb capital is so limited that relatively small amounts of capital ($2.5 to $3.5 billion per year additional from all sources) would probably satisfy the need." In a United Nations study the figure was set far higher but still only represented between 1 and 2 per cent of the total national income of the richer countries of the world. The United Nations experts based their estimates on the amount of money that would allow a "satisfactory" rate of growth; the other study dealt with the amounts that could be absorbed immediately. One figure may help to put the present investment of the poor countries in perspective: the sums spent each year under India's second five-year plan are about equal to the budget of the American Telephone & Telegraph Company.

Although much attention has been concentrated on the amount of money the rich countries should contribute for investment purposes, this is not the only issue. If the rich countries can produce goods more economically than the poor, should they make them available to the poor countries even though they cannot be paid for? Agriculture provides a good frame for examining the possibilities. Rapid scientific advance has placed the rich countries in a position where they can produce more food than is required for their own populations and for normal commercial exports. Good land is therefore left untilled or surpluses pile up while those in the poor countries go hungry. These nations would be willing to purchase the surplus food, but they are unable to earn sufficient foreign exchange to do so. In these circumstances are the rich countries justified in restricting production of crops that could increase the rate of growth in the poor countries? The United Nations Food and Agricultural Organization showed how an increase could be brought about: "In most underdeveloped countries there are unemployed and underemployed farmers and other workers. There are a number of projects which could be undertaken by putting these people to work with local materials and local resources, or with only small amounts of foreign equipment. This would speed their country's development and increase its productive ability by building roads, wells, dams, irrigation canals, schools, warehouses, processing plants, etc. But when unemployed people are put to work they have to be paid, and their increased purchases of food, clothing, etc. raise the level of demand. This increase in demand for consumer goods, coming into the market before the newly created facilities can expand production, would tend to cause inflation. This is where the surplus farm products from other countries would come in."

It is not surprising that the possibility of using farm surpluses abroad has attracted a good deal of attention. Adlai Stevenson has suggested that we must ". . . learn to use our surpluses of food and fibre as a major constructive resource in economic development, not as charity but as working capital—to enable men to divert their labor from agriculture to roads, dams, power stations and the like without creating an inflationary demand for food and clothing." Senator Hubert Humphrey of Minnesota went further, stating that the United States should use its "God-given abundance of food" and suggesting: "If the United States . . . cannot figure out what to do with our surplus . . . without wrecking the world economy . . . we are incapable of defending ourselves."

However, there will be a need for new attitudes and new institutions if it is to be possible to distribute aid of this type in large quantities. The disposal abroad of surplus American agricultural products led the chairman of the Australian Wheat Board to comment: "The United States is using the power granted by Congress to dump primary products in other countries. The terms of sales, financial considerations and ethics of fair trade are made subservient to the desperate desire to shift the responsibility for the caretaking and storing of products to countries other than the U.S.A." Similar charges are made in other countries about the effects of the American programs, while there are many in America who feel that the techniques used by other rich countries to dispose of their own surplus crops are no less reprehensible.

The standard of living in the various countries of the world is greatly affected by their ability to sell goods abroad; without exports a nation will not be able to obtain the foreign currency required to buy the imported goods it needs to continue producing. In present conditions any unusual export programs by foreign governments threaten the financial health, and in serious cases even the survival of the economy of other nations. As long as present institutions continue, it cannot therefore be expected that gift programs that interfere with commercial sales in the world market will be welcomed by other rich countries attempting to sell similar goods abroad.

We therefore reach a dilemma. The present system of free international competition will not allow the poor countries to earn sufficient foreign exchange to pay for the imports they need; thus the conditions of the poor countries can be expected only to get worse and the situation of the world to become more difficult. On the other hand, large transfers of aid are not possible within the present concept of international economic relations, for gifts from one country will inevitably cut into the sales of others. New mechanisms will, therefore, have to be developed that allow the transfer of goods from the rich to the poor countries without harming the position of other exporting countries.

By far the largest amount of aid since the war has been given on a bilateral basis. Foreign aid since the war has only too often been regarded as a method of securing the allegiance of a country to a given policy; an aim that events have often shown to be unrealizable. A comment by the London *Economist* brings out these facts: "Among the recipients of aid, some dislike the political strings attached to it; some rely on these strings too heavily, and are miffed when wealthy allies fail to meet all their demands; some have come to assume a moral right to larger benefits than they are getting. Among the donors, too, there is disenchantment: the feeling that some recipients are not merely ungrateful but insatiable; that some of them are unscrupulously playing both sides of the street and that others' professions of friendship are mere cupboard love."

There are, of course, exceptional relationships that are not covered by this statement, such as United States aid in Puerto Rico, British aid in some parts of the Commonwealth, and French aid in certain parts of Africa. But all too often aid has led to tension between the giver and the receiver. This is hardly surprising; the relationship between borrower and lender and between giver and receiver has never been a pleasant one, and when those concerned are not individuals but countries the possible sources of friction are greatly increased. One of the main causes of tension comes from the attempts of the rich countries to ensure that the money they give is "usefully" employed. This has often been regarded as an unwarranted interference in the internal affairs of the receiving country.

International aid has been used both by the West and more recently by the Russians as a weapon in the Cold War; a way to win friends and influence people. Funds have been exported in the hope that they will lead to alliances in the Cold War and will cause countries to adopt the economic system used in the giving or lending country. But the basis for these policies is largely wishful thinking; the poor countries cannot adopt either the pure communist or the pure capitalist doctrines, for they face problems that are unique in history; past doctrinal theorizing cannot help them.

It is, of course, unreasonable to expect that the aid programs of either bloc will be decided purely in terms of their utility in ensuring the progress of the poor countries as long as both blocs consider that they are engaged in a life-and-death struggle with an implacable opponent. In these circumstances it must be expected that aid programs, like all other policies, will be weighed to discover whether they will have a favorable or unfavorable effect on the position of the bloc. Nevertheless, all the countries concerned have stated that their aim is to help the poor countries without attaching strings to their aid, and that if tension were reduced they would be prepared to give more money through multi lateral aid.

The histories of the international agencies — whether of limited scope like the Colombo Plan or global like the United Nations and the World Bank — have been success stories. The amount of money disbursed by them has steadily increased, and the poor countries have proved willing to listen to unwelcome advice from these bodies, believing that it is based on their best interests, while they have been suspicious of the proposals of particular rich countries.

It is the consistent achievement of a relation of greater trust between the borrower and the lender and between the giver and the receiver that has led to a continuing increase in the volume of opinion claiming that more aid funds should be channeled through the international bodies. It is felt by many that foreign aid given only in this way can help to increase world unity, while bilateral aid will continue to be essentially divisive.

However, proposals for greatly increased programs of international aid have not been found acceptable by Russia, America, or the other rich countries. It is fair to say that the richer countries have accepted these projects only when the political pressure from the poor countries became overwhelming. Although certain new organizations have been set up in recent years, the sums they dispose of are restricted. The total planned capital for the Development Loan Fund, for example, will be only $1 billion, and it is planned that this should last for five years. By way of comparison it can be pointed out that the budget of New York City amounts to over $2 billion in a year.

However, too much emphasis should not be placed on the availability of funds, for this is not the most difficult problem. A greatly increased program of multilateral aid would be possible only after a reduction in international tension, and the consequent decrease in armaments expenditure that would follow would provide all the funds used. All the

funds that could be absorbed by the poor countries could
be provided without any major sacrifice. Less than ½ of
1 per cent of the total income of the rich countries is now
made available to the poor countries for economic development through grants, loans, and private investment. An
increase to 1 per cent over the next ten years would provide
all the funds the underdeveloped countries could absorb.
This is hardly an overwhelming burden: much less than
5 per cent of the annual increase in income of the rich
countries would be required. But if we are realistic we must
accept that, while the problems of the poor countries are
overshadowed by the East-West conflict, it is unlikely that
this question will receive the attention it deserves from the
top policy makers, who alone are capable of changing the
rules of the game of international trade. A rapid increase
in transfers would be possible only if such changes were
made, for an attempt to increase aid greatly within the
present institutional structure would inevitably lead to
serious tensions between rich countries.

Despite the fact that supplying the amount of resources
required by the poor countries would not require any major
sacrifice by the rich, there would be considerable difficulty
in establishing the principles on which the size of contributions should be based. Should they consist of a percentage
of the national income (figures that are unreliable for comparison between countries) or on some other criterion?
Under what conditions, if any, could countries claim that
their internal difficulties were so acute they could not contribute to the fund? How should the additional funds needed
each year be drawn from the contributing countries?

While it will be impossible to determine, with complete
equity, the size of contributions from the rich countries, it
will be even more difficult to distribute the benefit from the
aid fairly among the poor countries. In the past, two forms

of distribution have been used. The methods employed by single nations have been based largely on the political and military advantages that could be obtained by distributing wealth to certain countries. This principle would not be appropriate for international bodies. Nor will the principles at present adopted by the World Bank and other similar organizations be satisfactory in the future. There has been a tendency to demand that projects be presented in a highly developed form, and to deny requests that did not provide detailed specifications. While representatives of many poor countries agree that the discipline of providing complete information has been useful, they argue that it has tended to discriminate against the least wealthy and the most backward countries, who were unable to meet the requirements. As the amount of aid increases, the effects of this discrimination would become more unsatisfactory. Money should be distributed to all states in proportion to their needs; sums should accrue to all the poor countries. Those unable to use all the money allocated to them in one year should be assigned a larger number of experts who would initiate projects designed to increase their rate of growth.

One of the most violent controversies in recent years has been whether money should be given away in the form of grants or whether repayable loans should be made. The argument has become even more complex with the introduction of "soft" loans, which can be repaid in the currency of the borrower. Many experts in this field find difficulty in distinguishing between the reality behind "soft" loans and straightforward grants.

It is exceptionally difficult to sort out the arguments used to support grants and loans. Psychological, economic, and power factors are inextricably mixed. However, it would seem that the main arguments of those who favor loans are that the money sent abroad represents a sacrifice made by

those who did not use it themselves, and that they are therefore entitled to a return on the funds invested. In addition,
they argue that grants are psychologically unacceptable to
the poor countries because they carry the implication of
charity.

Those who argue that a large proportion of the transfers
should be in the form of grants would basically rest their
case on the deficit in the balance of payments that will continue in the poor countries for a long period. They argue
that any requirement that transfers should be repaid will
either hamper the rate of growth in the future or lead to
default on the loans; or that if neither of these two alternatives is found acceptable they can be avoided only by making additional loans that will enable the poor countries to
meet the payments on previous loans as they become due.
This, of course, does not mean that there is no place for
loans, particularly in business ventures, but it does suggest
that a substantial proportion of the money passing from the
rich countries to the poor should not have to be repaid.
The people favoring grants would generally agree that most
of the poor countries have regarded grants as humiliating
in the past. However, they point out that this reaction of
the poor countries has often been justified by the facts and
that if most aid were given through the United Nations and
other international organizations, the problem would
largely vanish.

Our approach to international trade and aid is still based
almost entirely on neoclassical static assumptions. We have
used little imagination to discover new areas in which the
interests of the rich and the poor countries coincided so that
we could build institutions that would benefit both the
rich and the poor countries. We have already seen that protection in the rich countries and free trade in the poor will
be best for the world taken as a whole, and will not hurt

the interests of either set of countries providing that changes are not made too rapidly. A further possibility that would aid both the rich and the poor countries would be an international countercyclical policy, designed to avoid the effects of slumps.

In the chapters on the rich countries we saw that a slump developed when the demand for goods was insufficient to take up all the available supply. Because the goods produced cannot be sold, manufacturers cut back production and lay off some workers. The impact of this change is unfavorable, for other manufacturers will tend to decrease production as their orders fall off; a cumulative decrease in the activity of the economy occurs. The problem in controlling business fluctuations, therefore, is to stop this cumulative process from gaining momentum; the generally accepted steps are a cheapening and loosening of credit policies in order to encourage private investment and also an increase in government investment. The problem is that neither of these solutions works very satisfactorily. A depression very naturally discourages investment within the economy, for it decreases the prospects of profit; it also decreases consumption, for those who have been thrown out of work are forced to limit their purchases. Those who still have jobs often take precautionary steps to build up their free reserves in case they too should be dismissed. It has also been found difficult to carry on government investment programs on a countercyclical basis, for few projects can be started just as a depression begins. Thus action within the country to stop the depression from developing is unlikely to be fully effective.

The depression is not confined, however, within the country in which it originates. In the same way as the orders of manufacturers within the country decline, so do the orders received by manufacturers, mining concerns, etc., outside the country. For the same reasons as applied in the country where the depression originated, production tends to fall off in outside countries. However, *unlike* the country where the depression originates and where the consumer and the manufacturer are unwilling to spend, the people in the poor countries let their purchases decline only because they are forced to do so. Thus the interests of the rich and the poor countries can be made to coincide. The rich countries are concerned to find ways in which the self-reinforcing nature of a recession can be broken; the poor countries wish to find a way to prevent the violent fluctuations in the values of their exports. It would therefore be practicable to set up a world stabilization fund that would compensate countries for decreasing export income as a depression developed.

Some might object that the International Monetary Fund is designed to deal with such problems. But the International Monetary Fund cannot create additional funds, it can only lend money that must be paid back at a later date. As the poor countries suffer from a permanent foreign-exchange shortage, they cannot afford to borrow extensively during a depression. The money paid by the World Stabilization Fund, however, would be in the form of grants; these grants would be effectively costless to the rich countries suffering from a depression, for the additional orders from the poor countries would use capacity otherwise idle.

Others would suggest that the slide in demand can be stopped by making additional resources available within the rich country, for we have seen that people are always willing to spend more money if it is available to them. Some steps can, of course, be taken toward this end; for example, by increasing unemployment benefits in time of depression. But any attempt to develop a countercyclical policy based on correlating taxes, etc., with the state of the business cycle would require such a high degree of intervention in the economy as to lead rapidly to complete central control.

The feasibility of a World Stabilization Fund will be denied for many reasons: among them the lack of adequate statistics, the impossibility of measuring proper compensation for declining exports, the danger that the poor countries would not be willing to see payments of this type decline as the depression ended. The feasibility of other recent new proposals in this field has been questioned on much the same grounds. It is, of course, true that without a greater degree of world unity than at present exists such a scheme is effectively impossible. However, it is equally true that it is only through new ideas that aim to discover where the interests of the rich and the poor countries can be made to harmonize that a viable economic system can be developed.

New methods of transferring resources must be found if the necessary level of aid is to be attained. We cannot be content with trade systems developed in an earlier age that reflect economic theories no longer valid. We must decide in principle that our aim is to transfer as much money to the poor countries as can usefully be employed there and then go to work to find methods of making these transfers with the minimum of friction.

In many of the poor countries time is working against all those who wish to ensure a fuller life for their inhabitants. If the increase in population is not to overwhelm all efforts, a revolution in attitudes must take place that will make the amount of aid given to the poor countries at the present time appear completely inadequate. We do not hesitate to spend large sums on social security within each rich country; can we deny our obligation to spend 1 per cent of the income of the rich countries to alleviate the far greater problems and poverty within the poor countries of the world?

XIII. *The Creation of a World Community of Nations*

We have attempted a re-examination of present world problems, paying particular attention to the difficulties resulting from changes in technology, social organization, and ideals. We have seen that the solutions devised for problems in the past are often unsuitable for present-day conditions and sometimes even aggravate the difficulties they were designed to meet. We have discovered that the possible rate of growth in productivity and production in the rich countries will be so great in coming years as to bring into question all the accepted values about work, consumption, and saving; that there will be a need for the development of new ways of using time. We have argued that in the poor countries the increasing population and the rising levels of tastes have made economic growth essential if starvation is to be avoided and the minimum aspirations of these countries satisfied. This overriding need for development will require that new methods of increasing the rate of growth are devised — methods that will often conflict with Western beliefs. The social aid made possible in the rich countries by their wealth will be impossible of application in the poor, while the methods of government of the poor countries must be designed to deal with their own particular problems. We saw that in all countries there would be a need for new systems of education that would allow individuals to keep up with the changing scene without mental breakdown and the society to adjust to changing circumstances.

In this section of the book we have discovered that free trade will not be appropriate for the poor countries in present conditions, but that a movement toward free trade by the rich could benefit both their own standard of living and that of the poor countries. We also saw that the rich countries were in a position where they could afford to take other steps that would increase the rate of growth in the poor countries. The amount of funds that could be absorbed immediately by the poor countries for investment was seen to be limited, but it was suggested that there was a need for gifts of agricultural and manufactured products that would enable unemployed and underemployed labor to be used, and reduce the possibility of famine. Such aid, however, was shown to depend upon the development of a different international atmosphere, one of co-operation rather than conflict. We are, therefore, led to consider the Cold War, which divides the world into two power blocs, according to differences in ideologies — differences exaggerated by the inability of both sides to understand that the position of the other is determined largely by conceptions of national interest and not by a desire for conflict.

Has it been realistic to consider the development of the rich and poor countries without examining the impact of the

Cold War? For the first time in the history of man the future can be considered without discussing the implications of a major war. Either the tension between the two existing power blocs is kept at levels at which it will not seriously affect economic development or there will eventually be a nuclear war. If this second alternative should occur, none of the comment made before the holocaust would be useful afterward, all conditions would be different; indeed many would argue there would be no real future.

Such a conclusion is sometimes denied. It is still suggested that either America or Russia or both could survive such a war and continue to prosper. It is argued that countries have been rebuilt after devastation in the past and that they will be able to recover from a nuclear attack in the same way. Such reasoning is wrong because the analogies are false. In the past, survivors of a war were able to take up their lives as best they could, for there was no residual effect of the attack. It is not generally realized that in previous wars devastation was limited. Despite the bombing of London during a long period in 1940, and further attacks by the buzz-bombs in 1944 and 1945, whole areas of the city were practically untouched, communications were hardly interrupted, and life continued. In a nuclear-bomb attack whole cities would be wiped out, with their road and rail junctions, different parts of the country would be entirely cut off from one another, people would be forced to remain in shelters for days or weeks until radioactivity diminished. The disruption of the intricate network of trade and industry is not difficult to visualize; it can be seen on a smaller scale each time a strike of transportation workers takes place. All these factors were recognized in figures suggesting that the casualties resulting from an attack on America might run as high as 80 per cent of the population; and in President Eisenhower's statement soon after his inauguration: "Since the advent of nuclear weapons, it seems clear that there is no longer any alternative to peace."

Is a nuclear war avoidable? From the point of view of America and her allies this question would seem to require an examination of Russian aims. But from the point of view of the Russians it is the aims of the Western allies that need examination. Each bloc is convinced of the aggressive intentions of the other, which they believe threaten the world's peace, while they themselves are willing for an accommodation on reasonable terms. This statement appears ridiculous; however, reality is not the objective truth, but the way in which the facts are perceived. Russia believes that she is threatened by the Western allies and that America's foreign bases are designed as spearheads of aggression. America and her allies are equally convinced that Russia is deterred from taking steps to destroy them only by their adequate armed strength. Each country proclaims its desire for peace while building up its armed might, and neither country believes the other. Adlai Stevenson put this clearly in an article in the New York *Times* written after his trip to Russia in 1958: ". . . I came away from this vibrant country with a much clearer feeling for the people's hunger for peace and dread of another war. I felt that the Russian people are really more fearful of the United States than we are of them, which is not hard to understand in view of our ring of air bases and the incessant propaganda about the hostility of the 'ruling cliques of the imperalist-capitalist powers.' Assuming we do not invite Soviet military adventure by our weaknesses, I do not fear a third world war. They know the terrible consequences; the very words 'world war' themselves are obsolete as a description of national suicide. But to avoid mutual suicide we are both piling up weapons to shoot at one another. It doesn't make sense . . ." *

While tension continues there is always a danger of war,

not because any country desires it, but because of a mistake — for example, a misreading of a radar screen that could result in missiles being dispatched in error. There is also a danger that both sides may maneuver themselves into a position where they cannot withdraw for fear of adverse public opinion. However, as both sides desire peace, tension can be reduced and there is fruitful ground for negotiation. Any step forward will help to convince the other bloc of good will. As tension decreases it will be realized that each side has legitimate interests it is trying to defend. We will find that agreement can be reached only if both sides are willing to negotiate.

In the future we will have to negotiate by examining a situation, realizing that the aims of those concerned will not usually be identical and that it will therefore be impossible for any country to gain the exact settlement it desires. Harmony can be preserved only if each side is willing to give up part of what it considers its legitimate interests. While the realities of power will always affect negotiations, it will be necessary to pay more attention to the advantages and disadvantages of certain steps for the world as a whole, rather than for each power to concentrate on its own interests and argue that settlements are wrong in so far as they are not protected.

Two problems will complicate attempts to reduce tension. The pace of scientific discovery is now so rapid that it is not inconceivable that one side would discover a new weapon that would make others obsolete or, at least, greatly decrease their effectiveness. As long as mutual suspicion continues to exist, it is idle to hope that the amount of scientific work devoted to warlike ends will greatly diminish. A reduction will be a result of the relaxation of tension and not its cause. The second difficulty is that, at present, national pride is so great that an order by a superior to launch hydrogen bombs on another country would be obeyed without hesitation; as a result no country can feel completely safe. It is only when populations believe in the brotherhood of all men and not only of those within national boundaries that the world can be free from the threat of war. When an order to devastate another country is generally disobeyed and indeed its issuance inconceivable, then the world can finally be safe.

Successful negotiations between West and East will require the development of new attitudes. It will be necessary to stop assuming that the opposite side deals only in propaganda, that all diplomatic notes of one side are serious proposals and those of the other designed to deceive. The world must seem less simple but at the same time the problems might become more soluble. Greater attention must be paid to the realities of the military situation, the new possibilities and new dangers that exist because of the practically unlimited powers of modern weapons. These developments have made many existing theories of international relations irrelevant.

The world is now too small and powers of destruction too great to allow conflicting loyalties to national states to continue. Our loyalty must be transferred to the world as a whole, if we are to meet the problems with which we are faced. If this loyalty is to have any reality, all the inhabitants of the world must be able to subscribe to a single set of beliefs. Each country at the present time has its own values, and it would be impossible to alter them drastically without destroying both the individual and society. The values of the world community can therefore be based only on the factor or factors that are common to all men.

It is really unnecessary to try to define these values; the words of the preamble to the United Nations Charter are more eloquent than any reformulation:

WE THE PEOPLES OF THE UNITED NATIONS
DETERMINED

to save succeeding generations from the scourge of war,
which twice in our lifetime has brought untold sorrow to
mankind, and

to reaffirm faith in fundamental human rights, in the dignity
and worth of the human person, in the equal rights of men
and women and of nations large and small, and

to establish conditions under which justice and respect for
the obligations arising from treaties and other sources of
international law can be maintained, and

to promote social progress and better standards of life in
larger freedom,

AND FOR THESE ENDS

to practice tolerance and to live together in peace with one
another as good neighbors, and

to unite our strength to maintain international peace and
security, and

to ensure by the acceptance of principles and institution of
methods that armed force shall not be used, save in the
common interest, and

to employ international machinery for the promotion of the
economic and social advancement of all peoples,

Have resolved to combine our efforts to accomplish these
aims.

The difficulty is not, therefore, to define the aims of a
world society but to develop a sense of loyalty to the aims
so described. If the ideals embodied in the charter were
to be realized, international aid would become the proper
and accepted course of action and war would become
inconceivable.

What must be the guidelines of the West in the revolutionary world in which we live? Certainly not the necessity
of preserving the capitalist system as we have known it in
the past. We must not struggle to retain values already
outdated in many ways; the free competitive model of the
economist no longer exists and cannot be resuscitated. The

free enterprise system—considerably modified—will continue to be the basis of Western society for many years; it is satisfactory, however, because it fits the desires and needs of these countries; it is not good in itself and should not be forced on others. As time passes it will be increasingly modified by policies at present called socialistic; much movement in this direction has already occurred. One of our greatest needs will be to cease using slogans and catchwords as substitutes for reflection. Both the voter and the politician are beginning to realize that actions are not good if they fit in a particular creed and bad if they do not, but that they must be evaluated in terms of the services they can render in a specific situation.

This book is based on one fundamental premise: all men have equal rights. I have tried to show that this equality does not, and should not, mean that each person should have the same education and training or that he must have the same beliefs and act in the same way as others; but it *does* require that the personality and individuality of each man, woman, and child be respected. I believe that there is only one vital difference between men, whether they want to improve the lot of others or only wish selfishly to better their own. Those who are concerned with the betterment of others must be supported by all men of good will; the use of labels such as democracy, totalitarianism, private enterprise, and state enterprise only disguise this essential truth. The methods used may still be considered unwise even when motives are good; however, our chance of influencing actions will be greater once it is recognized that the rulers of most countries are endeavoring to do their best in extremely difficult conditions.

Many in the present generation have been brought up to hate, their minds warped beyond repair; their beliefs cannot be revitalized. Unless immense efforts are made, it is inevitable that this process will be perpetuated in future generations. The time span in which we can work has been, and is being, shortened by the progress of science; where ten years could be taken to solve a problem a hundred years ago, it must now be solved in one; where a year could be taken, one now has a month. The task is immense, but I believe that the courage and the faith are there to meet it. Faced by a clear challenge, the ideal of world peace and the brotherhood of man could suffice to unite all the peoples of the world and to fuse their loyalties to their country into one to the world as a whole. Progress toward a world society is historically feasible; it moves with events.

A hundred years ago the creation of many of the present sovereign states would have seemed impossible; yet it has been successfully accomplished. Within these states there is still loyalty to the smaller geographical units in which one lives, but there is also a loyalty to the country as a whole. The creation of a world society does not mean the destruction of national pride, but the recognition of the stronger claim of all mankind. It has often been said in jest that the only thing that could unite the whole world would be a threat from outer space. United action is equally vital at the present time, for the threat to mankind's survival is just as great; however, we have been unable to see the scope of the problems because of their complexity.

The preservation of world peace depends on the willingness to avoid conflict and this in turn depends on the love one individual has for another, on the recognition of the essential humanity beneath the differing characteristics of each person. If peace is to be secured, a revival of toleration, understanding, and love will be necessary, and these virtues must be extended to fields where they have been usually considered irrelevant. Conflicts will always be imminent when individuals, societies, or nations are in contact; the problems can be resolved by strife or compromise. Only if a compromise is made and is directed, not by the balance of power, but by the underlying needs of all concerned, will further hatred be avoided.

We all have a common concern for the future of mankind. If all our discussions start from this basic principle and we do not allow slogans or shibboleths to interfere with our reasoning, societies can draw together. Agreement may still be difficult, but it will be possible to agree to differ. The situation will be recognized as a disagreement about the right means to follow rather than about ends. Divisions between societies and countries will not be exacerbated by a feeling of superiority of forms of government or by differences in customs. These will be recognized for what they are, part of the pattern of life, a variety that if understood aright could draw us together instead of tearing us apart.

Bibliography

In order to parallel the aim of this book, which introduces the reader to the problems of economic development, this bibliography provides a very limited list of the most interesting or important publications. It makes no attempt to satisfy the needs of those doing research in particular areas; bibliographies for this purpose are generally available.

PART I. THE POOR COUNTRIES

Peter Bauer. *Economic Analysis and Policy in Underdeveloped Countries.* Duke University Press, Durham, N. C. 1957.
Uses neoclassical economic theory to its best effect in explaining the problems of the poor countries.

Vera M. Dean. *The Nature of the Non-Western World.* New American Library, New York. 1957.
A study of the values and ways of life of the non-Western world.

Arthur Grimble. *A Pattern of Islands.* John Murray, London. 1952.

A volume by a British colonial administrator that lovingly describes the cultures on several islands in the Pacific.

Edward T. Hall. *The Silent Language.* Doubleday, Garden City, New York. 1959.

An examination of the many unexpected ways in which culture influences our behavior, and an attempt to develop theoretical tools to examine the problems encountered.

Albert O. Hirschmann. *The Strategy of Economic Development.* Yale University Press, New Haven. 1958.

A challenging analysis of the need for new thinking in the study of the problems of growth.

E. E. Hoyt. "The Impact of a Money Economy on Consumption Patterns," The Annals of the American Academy of Political and Social Science. May 1956.

Shows that reactions to increased income and employment opportunities would often be considered illogical by Western standards.

A. F. A. Husain. *Human and Social Impact of Technological Change in Pakistan.* Oxford University Press, Pakistan. 1956.

An examination of the effect of change on the welfare of individuals. Particularly important because of its use of the case-study.

Margaret Mead. *Cultural Patterns and Technical Change.* New American Library, New York. 1955.

Although this is one of the earliest studies of the effects of culture contact it is still among the most important; particularly in its examination of cross-cultural regularities.

Margaret Mead. *New Lives for Old: A Cultural Transformation—Manus 1928–1953.* William Morrow and Co. New York. 1956.

A study of the adaptation of a "primitive" society following contact with the West.

Julius K. Nyeere. "Africa Needs Time." *The New York Times Magazine.* March 27, 1960.

A brilliant study of the possibility of democracy and its wider meaning in Africa.

Robert Redfield. *A Village That Chose Progress*. University of Chicago Press, Chicago. 1950.
> An anthropologist returns to a Mexican-Indian village and describes the successful economic development that had taken place there since his previous visit and study.

Edward H. Spicer. *Human Problems in Technological Change*. Russell Sage Foundation, New York. 1952.
> A series of case studies of the effects of innovations—some successful, some not—with an analysis of the reasons for the results.

Elizabeth Marshall Thomas. *The Harmless People*. Alfred A. Knopf, New York. 1959.
> The utterly different way of life of the African bushmen is described in such a way as to make them come alive for the reader.

One periodical, *Economic Development and Cultural Change*, is particularly concerned with the problems examined in this part of the book. Many of its articles would be helpful in filling in the background.

PART II. THE RICH COUNTRIES

Clarence Edward Ayres. *Theory of Economic Progress*. University of North Carolina Press, North Carolina. 1944.
> A study of the effect of technology and increasing knowledge on economic growth.

Chester Irving Barnard. *Functions of the Executive*. Harvard University Press, Cambridge, Mass. 1938.
> The classic study of the role of the executive in a corporation.

Ralph J. Cordiner. *New Frontiers for Professional Managers*. McGraw-Hill, New York. 1956.
> An attempt by the chairman of General Electric to set up valid aims for a corporation in a changing world.

Fortune. Markets of the Sixties. Harpers, New York. 1960.
> A survey of the economic and social developments that can be expected in the 1960's.

J. K. Galbraith. *The Affluent Society*. Houghton-Mifflin Co., Boston, Mass. 1958.

Although it largely ignores the problems posed by the maldistribution of income within America and throughout the rest of the world, this book sets out clearly the consequences of a rising standard of living.

John Maynard Keynes. *The General Theory of Employment, Interest and Money*. Harcourt Brace & Co., New York. 1936.

The study of the reasons for depressions, which revolutionized economic analysis.

David Riesmann and others. *The Lonely Crowd*. Yale University Press, New Haven. 1950.

The relation of the individual to society in America.

Rockefeller Brothers Fund. *The Pursuit of Excellence*. Doubleday, Garden City, New York. 1958.

U. S. educational needs in the latter half of the twentieth century.

J. A. Schumpeter. *Capitalism, Socialism and Democracy*. Harpers, New York. 1942.

A study of the forces within the capitalist society and the changes they may cause.

Max Weber. *The Protestant Ethic and the Spirit of Capitalism*. Scribners, New York. 1958.

The often-quoted work by the German author that led to the present emphasis on the importance of the "Protestant Ethic" in development.

William H. Whyte. *The Organization Man*. Simon & Schuster, New York. 1956.

The threat institutionalized conformity poses to economic development and to the values of society.

PART III.   INTERNATIONAL RELATIONS

Chester Bowles. *Ideas, People and Peace*. Harpers, New York. 1958.

A study of the problems of the poor countries and the possibility of a "creative American response."

Pearl S. Buck and Carlos P. Romulo. *Friend to Friend*. John Day, New York. 1958.
A candid exchange between an American friend of Asia and an Asian friend of America.

Paul G. Hoffmann. "One Hundred Countries—One and One Quarter Billion People." Committee for International Economic Growth, Washington. 1960.
A proposal for the enlargement of foreign aid to double the rate of growth in the poor countries as a whole. The sums suggested are far smaller than those proposed in this book and would seem to be insufficient.

Emmet John Hughes. *America the Vincible*. Doubleday, Garden City, New York. 1959.
A study of the controlling ideas in American foreign policy during the last decade and their relevance in a changing world.

George E. Kennan. *Russia, the Atom and the West*. Harpers, New York. 1958.
The elaboration of Kennan's argument that the present international situation is unstable and that both Russia and America should withdraw their forces from Europe.

Henry A. Kissinger. *Nuclear Weapons and Foreign Policy*. Harpers, New York. 1957.
An examination of the implications for American policy of the availability of nuclear weapons.

John D. Montgomery. *The Politics of American Aid*. Council on Foreign Relations, New York. To be published.
A study of the political realities which will affect decisions on foreign aid in both the rich and the poor countries.

Gunnar Myrdal. *Rich Lands and Poor: The Road to World Prosperity*. Harpers, New York. 1957.
Explores the inadequacies of present economic theory and also the effect of Western value systems on economic growth in the poor countries.

Philip Noel-Baker. *Arms Race: Program for World Disarmament*. Oceana Publications, New York. 1958.
A study by the Nobel prize winner of the conditions under which world disarmament would be possible.

Rockefeller Brothers Fund. *Foreign Economic Policy for the Twentieth Century.* Doubleday, Garden City, New York. 1958.
A study of present trade-aid methods and suggestions for new developments.

Adlai Stevenson. *Friends and Enemies, What I learned in Russia.* Harpers, New York. 1959.
A report on a trip to Russia in 1958.

Arnold Wolfers, ed. *Alliance Policy in the Cold War.* Johns Hopkins Press, Baltimore. 1959.
The relevance and utility of alliances in the present situation.

A series of studies has recently been completed for the Senate Foreign Relations Committee covering all aspects of U. S. foreign relations. They will be published in book-form in the fall of 1960.

DATE DUE